Credible Signs of Christ Alive

Credible Signs of Christ Alive

Case Studies from the Catholic Campaign for Human Development

John P. Hogan

A SHEED & WARD BOOK

ROWMAN & LITTLEFIELD PUBLISHERS, INC.
Lanham • Boulder • New York • Oxford

A SHEED & WARD BOOK

ROWMAN & LITTLEFIELD PUBLISHERS, INC.

Published in the United States of America
by Rowman & Littlefield Publishers, Inc.
A wholly owned subsidary of the Rowman & Littlefield Publishing Group, Inc.
4501 Forbes Boulevard, Suite 200, Lanham, Maryland 20706
www.rowmanlittlefield.com

PO Box 317
Oxford
OX2 9RU, UK

This book is published with the generous support of the Catholic Campaign for Human
Development, United States Conference of Catholic Bishops, 3211 4th Street, N.E.,
Washington, DC 20017-1194 (202) 541-3000. To visit the Catholic Campaign for Human
Development on the world wide web: http://www.nccbuscc.org/the CCHD

British Library Cataloguing in Publication Information Available

Library of Congress Cataloging-in-Publication Data

Hogan, John P.
  Credible signs of Christ alive : case studies from the Catholic Campaign for Human
  Development / John P. Hogan.
      p. cm.
  Includes bibliographical references and index.
  ISBN 0-7425-3166-X (alk. paper)—ISBN 0-7425-3167-8 (pbk. : alk. paper)
  1. Church and social problems—Catholic Church—Case studies. 2. Social justice—
United States—Case studies. 3. Campaign for Human Development—Case studies. I. Title.

HN37.C3 H582 2003
361.7'5'08822—dc21   2003006550

Printed in the United States of America

To all those on the margins and to those who work with CCHD on their behalf.

Contents

Foreword

I consider it a great honor to offer these brief opening words as the readers of this book embark on a pilgrimage of faith and of subsequent future action in the work of justice. By articulating clear theological principles and depicting powerful human experiences, the author challenges us to reflect on ways that members of low-income communities throughout this country can and do embody the Gospel of Jesus by liberating themselves from unjust social structures and becoming continually more conscious of their own inherent human dignity as children of God. Truly, the prophetic mandate to "bring glad tidings to the poor" (Lk 4:18), is forcefully re-issued through this book and demands a response of Catholics and all people of goodwill.

In sage fashion, John Hogan adopted a methodology based in actual experience. By inviting the reader to walk in the shoes of those who are caught in the cycle of poverty, he unfolds the principles and beliefs of Catholic Social Teaching in a tangible and engaging manner.

I was especially pleased to support the author's proposal to focus on "case models" of projects supported by the Catholic Campaign for Human Development (CCHD). When they established the Campaign in 1970, the bishops of the United States urgently appealed to the Catholic faithful to move beyond the traditional works of charity, necessary as they are, in order to accompany directly low-income people as they strive to quench their thirst for justice. Since that time, Catholics have donated hundreds of millions of dollars to support thousands of community-based, self-help projects that are initiated and led by poor people themselves. Through its educational efforts, the Campaign also has awakened among many Catholics in the United States an interest in the plight of the poor and a determination to join them in solidarity as they change oppressive social structures.

As the National Director of CCHD, I have been privileged to visit many of the empowered, low-income people depicted in this book and countless others. Their stories make the tenets of the Catholic faith come alive for me and hopefully will do the same for the readers of this book. In their tireless efforts to build a better future for their children, they collaborate with God in building up the Reign of Peace and Justice inaugurated by Jesus who remains present among us through the force of the Spirit.

At the outset of the twenty-first century, Pope John Paul II reminded us that "efforts for justice, the struggle against every oppression, and the safeguarding of the dignity of the person are not expressions of philanthropy motivated solely by membership in the human family." He insisted, instead, that "they are choices and acts that have a profoundly religious inspiration, they are true and proper sacrifices that are pleasing to God." (Pope John Paul II, Address at General Audience, January 10, 2001). I have no doubt that the struggles of low-income people so cogently presented in this book can truly be counted among those "pleasing sacrifices." May God continue to accompany them and us as we attempt to discern the credible signs of Christ in our midst.

—Rev. Robert J. Vitillo, Executive Director,
Catholic Campaign for Human Development

Preface

This small volume introduces readers to the work of the Catholic Campaign for Human Development (CCHD), the domestic anti-poverty and social justice program sponsored by the United States Conference of Catholic Bishops. CCHD's mission is to confront the root causes and structure of poverty by funding local and regional self-help community-controlled projects. The Campaign's work focuses on community organization, economic development, and education for justice. CCHD makes a special effort to fund projects of and for the truly needy among us, increasingly the working poor. The work of the Campaign is supported by an annual collection taken up nationwide in Catholic parishes, usually the weekend before Thanksgiving.

To be eligible for funding, projects must satisfy three criteria: (1) Organizations must be working to bring about institutional change by attacking basic social, economic, and political causes of poverty. The goal is permanent, sustainable change; (2) the principal beneficiaries of the project must be poor people—at least 50 percent of participants must be from the low-income community; and (3) poor people must have the dominant voice in the project. At least 50 percent of those who plan and implement the projects, e.g., the board of directors, must be persons who are involuntarily poor.

These criteria as well as CCHD's stated priority of solidarity between the poor and the non-poor will be made evident in a series of six project profiles. A case study and reflection approach is used with the explicit intention of reaching a broad spectrum of parish and classroom audiences. Effort has been made to employ a popular style and, whenever possible, to avoid, or at least to explain, technical language. Footnotes are not used; references to Catholic Social Teaching and other sources are cited in the text. Project reports, public documents, and newspaper accounts were consulted. Additional works that were helpful in unpacking or explaining the cases are included under "Optional Further Study."

Most importantly, the author spent time in each of the communities and did extensive interviews with project participants. The reader, in turn, is invited into those conversations with low-income working men and women as well as with young people who have gained from this Catholic campaign against poverty and powerlessness. For too many of us the poor remain hidden, but one cannot fail to be moved when the poor are given a face, a name, and a voice. The projects described below do just that. They tell the story behind the poverty statistics and the hope behind the headlines. The CCHD's lens of faith brings the story of poverty into focus. The case studies may also be read as commentaries on one of the defining themes of Pope John Paul's papacy—building solidarity between the poor and non-poor.

The book and the case studies are formatted for use by parish adult education programs. Each week one case study could be read and discussed. This format, however, does not preclude other classroom use. The first chapter presents a brief introduction to Catholic Social Teaching and creates a context for the CCHD projects. The case studies in subsequent chapters are broken down into a setting which tells the story of the group and the issues they face. To the extent possible, project participants are left to speak in their own voices. To protect privacy, often only first names are used; in a few instances names have been changed. A summary of accomplishments and project impact is provided. A reflection, which points out the biblical roots and Catholic Social Teaching involved in the project, accompanies each case and is followed by discussion questions, suggested parish (or classroom) action, and optional readings. The approach is designed to emphasize the crucial Catholic connection between the spiritual life and a commitment to social justice. The case studies are followed by two appendices: "Poverty U.S.A.: The State of Poverty in America" and excerpts from "Being Neighbor: The Catechism and Social Justice." These two summary statements, available on the CCHD website, serve as a final reflection on the cases.

In each of the projects profiled, an effort was made to draw out of the story the rich tradition of Catholic Social Teaching—both the papal encyclicals and the relevant statements of the U.S. Bishops. Quotations from this tradition are sprinkled throughout the text and should provoke a dialogue with the case being studied. It is also the hope of the author that the quotes will entice the reader to dig deeper into this exciting legacy. I have found Thomas Massaro's *Living Justice: Catholic Social Teaching in Ac-*

tion to be a very helpful companion volume and have referenced his treatment of themes and principles in each of the cases.

Some words of thanks are certainly in order. The staff of CCHD was very helpful in the selection of the projects to be studied. They were also most patient in responding to my numerous questions. Rev. Robert J. Vitillo, the executive director, and Mary Wright, the education coordinator, have been exceptionally supportive through the whole project, which included a travel grant that made visiting these projects possible. Thanks are also due to a number of careful readers who offered suggestions on early drafts of the cases. A special note of gratitude is owed to Maura Donohue for her assistance with style, editing, and typing. Thanks to Jeremy Langford, Editorial Director, and the staff of Sheed & Ward for bringing this manuscript to publication. All royalties from the sale of this book will go to CCHD.

Most of all I want to express my deepest gratitude to the men and women involved in each of the cases studied. They shared stories of suffering, faith, and hope. And in spite of some dismal circumstances, faith and hope prevailed. This project was launched at a planning meeting with the CCHD staff on the sad and frightening day of September 11, 2001. It is coming to an end as all of us in the Church face up to a sad and frightening scandal and our nation faces terrorism and the possibility of all-out war. It is no exaggeration to say that we live in a time when we desperately need credible signs of Christ alive. Across the United States, CCHD and the groups it funds have given us some glowing examples.

Introduction

Catholic Social Teaching and the Catholic Campaign for Human Development

Before we turn to our case studies, it will be of value to create a context for the reader. The project profiles are best understood when viewed through the faith-justice lens of CCHD. That lens helps us to bring into focus the face of America's poor with the face of the poor revealed to us in the life, death, and resurrection of Jesus.

Although not all of the cases studied have direct church links, all relate closely, as we will see, to biblical roots and Catholic Social Teaching. This introductory chapter will briefly outline something of those roots and teachings. But the reader is reminded, even cautioned, at this point, of the basic premise of the case-study approach: beginning with real life stories is always more informative and more exciting and usually the best way to ignite the Catholic sacramental imagination. Our goal should be to put ourselves into the story—to the extent that we can—and identify with the people in the cases. But first, let us begin with a story familiar to all of us about a tough stretch of road between Jerusalem and Jericho. As we will see, the same kind of road runs right across our country from Camden, New Jersey, to Los Angeles, California.

GOOD SAMARITAN: DO-GOODER OR RISK TAKER?

The lawyer tested Jesus with the age-old and ageless question, "Teacher, what must I do to inherit eternal life?" When Jesus' surprising response united love of God with love of neighbor, the questioner became defensive and self-righteous. "And who is my neighbor?" (Stoutzenberger, *The Christian Call to Justice and Peace*, pp. 8–10).

> Jesus replied, "A man fell victim to robbers as he went down from Jerusalem to Jericho. They stripped and beat him and went off leaving him half-dead. A priest happened to be going down that road, but when he saw him, he passed by on the opposite side. Likewise, a Levite came to the place, and when he saw him, he passed by on the opposite side. But a Samaritan traveler who came upon him was moved with compassion at the sight. He approached the victim, poured oil and wine over his wounds and bandaged them. Then he lifted him up on his own animal, took him to an inn and cared for him. The next day he took out two silver coins and gave them to the innkeeper with the instruction, 'Take care of him. If you spend more than what I have given you, I shall repay you on my way back.' Which of these three, in your opinion, was neighbor to the robber's victim?" He answered, "The one who treated him with mercy." Jesus said to him, "Go and do likewise" (Lk 10:30–37).

At this point probably most of us fast-forward to identify with the Samaritan but fail to really grasp the twist Jesus is giving to his parable. Most of us have some sense of what it means to be a victim. We might be scared stiff in certain city neighborhoods. We might have been laid-off in a corporate downsizing or had our pension plans vaporized overnight. We might even have been mugged walking home from the bus stop. In short, we can readily identify with the "help" part of Jesus' parable. Why not stop and help the poor guy? But the parable is about more than helping a victim on a dark street or highway. It is about more than the dilemma of stopping or dialing 911. It concerns the much broader issues of human solidarity and what Pope John Paul II refers to as entrenched "structures of sin." It is about systemic change, a way of being that promotes the good of every individual.

The story confronts us with numerous questions and the potential for endless application to our own times. Was the situation a question of charity or was there a longer-range issue of justice? Was this a chance occurrence or were travelers easy targets on a road controlled by gangsters? Who was responsible for safety? Most importantly, why were the people with the power, means, and authority—the community, religious, and government leaders—unwilling to respond? Apparently, they believed they couldn't help the bleeding man because his blood might contaminate them and render them unworthy to worship in the temple, according to the purity laws of the times. Institutional, religious, and national structures made them close their eyes and slink to the other side of the road. It is easy for us to pass judgment on these men, but what would we have done in the same situation? What do we do in our own lives to reach out to those in need? Are there subtle sinful structures of racial, religious, national, or class prejudice that lead us to be like the men in the story?

The parable is meant to confront us with stark contrast. If eternal life is tied up with love of neighbor and victim—which side are we on? Are we willing to stand by and stand up for victims? Are we willing to risk and share some of our resources, power, and authority? Unfortunately, "Samaritan" has crept into our vocabulary as "do-gooder" but clearly Jesus had something much stronger in mind. The Samaritan—a victim himself as a member of an outcast minority in his time—takes a risk and opts for the victim, a trait repeated over and over in our case studies. Jesus' meaning reaches all the way back to the prophets and forward to modern Catholic Social Teaching. We are all in some ways victims but God's justice through Christ somehow clings to us. For Jesus, as for Jeremiah, to know God is to do justice (cf. Jer 22:13–16). God is on the side of the victim—the poor, the outcast. But that doesn't mean he's not on our side. It means rather that God is pushing us to see, understand, and identify with the less fortunate in our society. That is the meaning of the Church's "option for and with the poor." In a very real sense it is a call to conversion. It is also a twenty-first century insight into Jesus' challenge to the lawyer, "Go and do likewise."

Most of us probably want to "do likewise," we are just not sure how to go about it. Often the hardest thing about following Christ is translating good intentions into deeds. Catholic Social Teaching offers some guidelines. But as has often been said, Catholic Social Teaching is "our best kept secret." That unfortunately is still too true. Nonetheless, the word, as our case studies indicate, is getting out. For over thirty years, CCHD has put flesh on the bones of Catholic Social Teaching helping poor people become empowered and design solutions to their own problems. At the same time the Campaign has fostered partnerships and solidarity with those with greater access to resources and power. The best-kept secret is at least being whispered. The gospel call to justice is working to break the cycle of poverty. Indeed, we can as a community "go and do likewise."

BIBLICAL ROOTS OF JUSTICE

As one reads and reflects on the case studies in the following chapters, it is very easy to project biblical images onto the men and women and the scenes described. In a few instances, I have done just that. The very revelation of God in the Old Testament, beginning with Genesis, takes place in a call to responsibility and justice. The Hebrew word used for *justice* relates to defense of the weak, the freeing of the oppressed. The story of the Exodus is key and a model for community organizing—complete with training—". . . I will assist both you and [Aaron] in speaking and will teach the two of you what you are to do" (Ex 4:15).

[Community Organizing] is a values-based process by which people—most often low-and moderate-income people previously absent from decision-making tables—are brought together in organizations to jointly act in the interest of their "communities" and the common good.

The term "values-based" refers to values that form the basis of CO theory and practice. For most community organizers and . . . groups, the values include: community, solidarity, equality, freedom, justice, the dignity of the individual, respect for differences, civility, and political democracy. (Larry Parachini and Sally Covington, *Community Organizing Toolbox: A Funder's Guide to Community Organizing*, Washington, D.C.: Neighborhood Funders Group, 2001, pp. 11 and 41, fn 9.)

The poverty, harsh labor, and humiliation which the Jews suffered in Egypt present a horrible and almost hopeless picture. But the spark of hope is never extinguished, God awakens the call to leadership in Moses. It is interesting to note that like the leaders in our cases, and probably, like most of us, leadership begins with lots of butterflies in the stomach. Moses too had that queasy feeling when he had to stand up for what was right. He was hesitant and stammering. "Who am I that I should go to the Pharaoh and lead the Israelites out of Egypt?" (Ex 3:11). "If you please Lord, send someone else" (Ex 4:13). But Moses rises to the call. That call to freedom, however, is also a call to responsibility and is, indeed, threatening not only to the powerful—the Pharaoh—but also to the powerless—the Hebrews themselves. The Exodus account is very candid and realistic, not unlike the stories which follow. In many ways the ancient Hebrews are a symbol of the reluctance we all experience when faced with real freedom and responsibility. But as the men and women in our case studies show us, the epitome of sin is giving in and giving up. That is denying one's humanity and denying God—idolatry. Today, if we are candid, we can imagine accusing Moses, the "activist," of stirring up the poor people who really were content with their lot. Indeed, Jesus too would fall prey to the same charge. The Scriptures are a mirror to read the signs of our own times.

When Israel forgets its own history and God's call to justice, the prophets—especially Amos, Isaiah, and Jeremiah—take up their role as social conscience. True religion cannot be reduced to ritual or lip service.

> Away with your noisy songs!
> I will not listen to the melodies of your harps.
> But if you would offer me holocausts
>   then let justice surge like water,
>   and goodness like an unfailing stream (Am 5:23–24).

> This, rather, is the fasting that I wish:
>   releasing those bound unjustly . . .
> Setting free the oppressed . . .
> Sharing your bread with the hungry,
>   sheltering the oppressed and the homeless;
> Clothing the naked when you see them,
>   and not turning your back on your own (Is 58:6–7).

Liturgy and sacrament come alive and are made manifest in works of charity and justice. Religion is animated by service.

Jesus built on this tradition with his message of the Kingdom of God. His first preaching echoed Isaiah.

> The Spirit of the Lord is upon me,
>   because he has anointed me
>   to bring glad tiding to the poor.
> He has sent me to proclaim liberty to captives
>   and recovery of sight to the blind,
>   to let the oppressed go free,
> and to proclaim a year acceptable to the
>   Lord (Lk 4:18–20).

These same themes reverberate throughout all of the gospels and the letters of St. Paul. Jesus is "the justice of God." He was clearly a critic, a troublemaker, and a disturber of the peace who must have really riled the local authorities when he said that the Kingdom of God had already begun!

To return to the Good Samaritan story, it is not clear that the lawyer caught the real meaning of "neighbor" but we don't have any excuses for missing the point. Solidarity and service are woven throughout the great lessons of the New Testament: the Beatitudes (Lk 6:20–26); Lazarus and the rich man (Lk 16:19–31); the washing of the feet (Jn 1:12–20); the final judgment (Mt 25:31–46).

Jesus' death on the cross is the consequence of a life in the radical service of justice and love, a consequence of his option for the poor and outcast human beings, of a choice for his people that suffered exploitation and manipulation. Within an evil world, any commitment to justice and love is perilous. (Edward Schillebeeckx, *Church: The Human Story of God*, New York: Crossroad, 1990, p. 125.)

The lessons might seem harsh or demanding, but the meaning is clear: ignoring the sufferings of the poor not only hurts the poor; in the long run, it hurts us all. That is the thrust of Pope John Paul's message on solidarity between the poor and the non-poor. In his first encyclical *Redeemer of Humankind*, 1979, no. 13, he set the tone for that solidarity by reminding us that "through his incarnation the Son of God united himself to each one of us." If only we could grasp Christ's identification with all of humanity—and especially the poor and the vulnerable—we could move in faith to a real human solidarity.

CATHOLIC SOCIAL TEACHING

The biblical roots of justice and God's call to human solidarity, especially solidarity with the poor as manifested in the Incarnation, involve serious ethical, economic, social, and political implications. Being Catholic means being socially responsible. We are called "to work for justice; to serve those in need; to pursue peace; and to defend life, dignity and rights of all sisters and brothers. This is the call of Jesus, the challenge of the prophets, and the living tradition of the Church" (U.S. Catholic Bishops, *A Century of Social Teaching*, 1990, 1).

This call to action and service is spelled out in a series of Papal documents and Bishops' statements which form modern Catholic Social Teaching. The major documents of modern Catholic Social Teaching are included in the table below.

Pope Leo XIII, *On the Condition of Labor*, 1891
Pope Pius XI, *The Reconstruction of the Social Order*, 1931
Pope John XXIII, *Christianity and Social Progress*, 1961
Pope John XXIII, *Peace on Earth*, 1963
Vatican Council II, *The Church in the Modern World*, 1965
Pope Paul VI, *The Development of Peoples*, 1967
Pope Paul VI, *A Call to Action*, 1971
World Synod of Bishops, *Justice in the World*, 1971
Pope Paul VI, *Evangelization in the Modern World*, 1975
Pope John Paul II, *On Human Work*, 1981
U.S. Catholic Bishops, *The Challenge of Peace*, 1983
U.S. Catholic Bishops, *Economic Justice for All*, 1986
Pope John Paul II, *On Social Concern*, 1987
Pope John Paul II, *The Hundredth Year*, 1991
Pope John Paul II, *The Gospel of Life*, 1995
Pope John Paul II, *Ecclesia in America*, 1999

Catholic Social Teaching began in the late nineteenth century with Pope Leo XIII's *On the Condition of Labor* (1891) which took up questions related to the harsh economic conditions and abuse of workers brought about by the Industrial Revolution. The encyclical supported the workers' right to organize and join unions and the need for a "family" or "just" wage. This legacy continued through Vatican II and the U.S. Bishops' *Economic Justice for All* (1986) and John Paul II's *On Social Concern* (1987) and *The Hundredth Year* (1991). The recent encyclicals of Pope John Paul II broaden the legacy to deal with structures of sin, global injustice, the growing gap between rich and poor, and the contemporary dangers of consumerism.

Pope John Paul's social message embodies new elements which have come to the fore since the Second Vatican Council, 1961–1965. These include a social or structural dimension to sin and a "preferential option for the poor and the vulnerable." What the Pope refers to as "structures of sin" are rooted in "personal sin and thus always linked to the concrete acts of individuals who introduce these structures, consolidate them and make them difficult to remove. And thus they grow stronger, spread and become the source of other sins, and so influence people's behavior" (*The Social Concerns of the Church*, 1988, no. 36). Discrimination against racial minorities would be the prime example for Americans. But overall, the realization of the social and structural dimensions of sin cries out for a preferential response.

These two teachings, the social or structural dimension of sin and the option for the poor, have pointed the Church toward a more active stance which seeks to empower poor people themselves. Solidarity is the key.

> Positive signs in the contemporary world are the growing awareness of solidarity of the poor among themselves, their efforts to support one another, and their public demonstrations on the social scene which, without recourse to violence, present their own needs and rights in the face of the inefficiency or corruption of public authorities. By virtue of her own evangelical duty, the Church feels called to take her stand beside the poor, to discern the justice of their requests, and to help satisfy them, without losing sight of the good of groups in the context of the common good. (Pope John Paul II, *On Social Concerns*, 1987, no. 39.)

> The "cries of those who are poor" in our society demand new and renewed commitment to systemic social change through organizing, community outreach, legislative networks, racial reconciliation, social policy development, coalition- building, and public and private sector partnerships for economic development. (U.S. Bishops, *In All Things Charity*, 1999, 32.)

Two additional quotes capture well the social commitment of the Church and the intimate linkage between faith and justice.

The joys and hopes, the sorrows and anxieties of the women and men of this age, especially those who are poor or in any way oppressed—these are the joys and hopes, the sorrows and anxieties of the followers of Christ. (Vatican II, *The Church and the Modern World*, 1965, no. 1.)

Action on behalf of justice and participation in the transformation of the world fully appear to us as a constitutive dimension of the preaching of the Gospel, or, in other words, of the Church's mission for the redemption of the human race and its liberation from every oppressive situation. (World Synod of Bishops, *Justice in the World*, 1971, no. 6.)

The challenge embodied in these quotes is framed by a set of principles and themes which have been distilled from scripture, history, and Catholic reflection on ethics, economics, politics, and law. These basic themes of Catholic Social Teaching will be fleshed out in each of our case studies. The following brief preview alerts the reader to some basic concepts.

1. *Life and dignity of the human person.* Every one of us is made in God's image. The human person is central. Basic dignity is not something we earn; it is a gift of God. No matter what TV, pop culture, fashion, the stock market, or the government say, people are sacred and more important than things.

2. *Call to family, community, and participation.* How we organize society, laws, economics, and public policy affects the integrity and well-being of individuals and families. We depend on one another. We need to participate in the decisions that affect us; when one suffers, we all suffer. *Subsidiarity*, a key concept, is related to *participation* and means that decisions about governance and economics should be made as closely as possible to the people most directly affected. Families, neighborhoods, community organizations, and small businesses should have a strong voice. But when necessary for the *common good* larger government entities should be ready to step in and assist.

3. *Rights and responsibilities.* Fundamental human rights need to be protected. Each person has a right to food, shelter, health care, education, and employment. Coupled with these rights, however, is our individual and collective *responsibility* to help meet the needs of one another and society as a whole.

4. *Option for and with the poor and vulnerable.* The test of our society's real moral worth is how we treat the most vulnerable people in our midst. Catholic tradition affirms Jesus' teaching on the Last Judgment. "For I was hungry and you gave me food, I was thirsty and you gave me drink, a stranger and you welcomed me. . . . Amen, I

say to you, what you did not do for one of those least ones, you did not do for me" (Mt 25:35–45). Working with the poor and vulnerable is a special duty.

5. *Dignity of work and the rights of workers.* The dignity of the person and the dignity of work are intimately connected. The economy exists to serve people, not the other way around. The basic rights of workers must be protected: the right to organize and join a union, the right to a living wage, and adequate benefits such as health insurance.

6. *Solidarity.* The teaching of the gospel calls us to love and serve our neighbor but to expand that concept of neighbor beyond family, national, racial, and religious limits. We are called to be one human family and in a special way to manifest our solidarity with those less fortunate. This notion of solidarity is a central theme of John Paul II and is a contemporary way of expressing St. Paul's image of the "Body of Christ" in the age of globalization.

7. *Care for God's creation.* From the opening lines of the Bible, we are called upon to live in harmony with one another and with God's creation. *Stewardship* of the environment means concern for issues such as air and water pollution, exploitation of animals, increased use of pesticides and fertilizers, global warming, and recycling of materials. Care of the earth is a requirement of our faith.

The above seven themes are a popular thumbnail sketch of Catholic Social Teaching. However, we should not be content with simply checking off a list of themes or principles. Principles can sound too idealistic or academic. Moreover, the application of broad principles in complicated economic and political situations is a very delicate matter. Massaro quotes Pope Paul VI:

> In the face of such widely varying situations, it is difficult for us to utter a unified message and to put forward a solution which has universal validity. Such is not our ambition nor our mission. It is up to the Christian communities to analyze with objectivity the situation which is proper to their own country, to shed on it the light of the Gospel's unalterable words and to draw principles of reflection, norms of judgment and directives for action from the social teaching of the Church. (Pope Paul VI, *A Call to Action*, 1971, no. 4.)

Massaro goes on to say that these "sentences contain much wisdom" (Massaro, pp. 107–108). Indeed, as we will see, the same kind of wisdom is evident in the cases below. Principles cannot be applied in a "one-size-fits-all" fashion.

Very often the reaction to the Church's social teaching and to the political and economic implications of the gospel is either one of ignorance—"I didn't know that"—or defensive discomfort—"What is the Church doing messing around in politics and business?" Both are unfortunate reactions and not far removed from the parable of the Good Samaritan. But these reactions usually change when principles are seen and understood in practice. That is what this book hopes to accomplish.

CASE STUDIES

It is in the conversations with project participants and the analysis of their own situations that human dignity, workers' rights, solidarity, the option for the poor, and concern for the environment came alive for me and revealed the human face of God. The human story—the human struggle—opens the way to shared meaning and free discussion where we can hear and better understand the stranger, the poor, the marginalized. It is only in this way that we get to know who our neighbor is and better understand what is really happening on that tough stretch of highway to Jericho.

Many times during my visits to the CCHD projects, the beautiful reflections of John Kavanaugh in *Faces of Poverty, Faces of Christ* came back to me:

There is a poverty which is not blessed
It is a curse . . .
It can crush the spirit . . .
Christ came not to bless this poverty, but to change it . . .
Finally, so much would he want this dehumanizing poverty changed, he
revealed that our response to such degradation would be the very condition of
our entry into his reign . . .
So much did he want the sufferings of these poor attended to that he took upon
himself their skin and bones
And told us we would be attending to him

The projects reflected on in the next six chapters cut across the United States and represent a broad range of the working poor—whites, African-Americans, Latin Americans, and a variety of immigrant groups including Africans, Asians, Hispanics, and Russians. The case studies focus on CCHD's thirty-year history in community organization as well as its more recent emphasis on economic development. A clear concern was to link the cases to CCHD's emphasis on Education for Justice and its poverty awareness campaign, PovertyUSA.org. Both efforts reach out to the nonpoor. This educational component is essential to CCHD's mission and is highlighted in the 1970 founding resolution. "The poor have not chosen poverty. Poverty is the result of circumstances over which the poor themselves have little or no control. We hope through the Campaign for Human Development to impress the facts on the non-poor and to effect in them a conversion of heart, a growth in compassion and sensitivity to the needs of their brothers [and sisters] in want" (*Resolution on the CCHD*, NCCB, 1970).

The first case describes the Delmarva Poultry Justice Alliance and its effort to bring together small chicken farmers with poor, immigrant poultry workers to organize and fight for workers' rights, better working coalitions, and more just contract arrangements.

The Northern Virginia suburbs of Washington, D.C., is the locale of the second case study. Working largely with low-income, new immigrants, the Tenants and Workers Support Committee organized and won the Alexandria City Council's support for a living wage for all city government contract workers.

The third case chronicles the decades-long organizing struggle of the Camden Churches Organized for People and the battle to rebuild Camden, New Jersey, one of the poorest cities in the country. Their organizing effort eventually won massive support from the governor and state legislature.

Southwest Iowa with its rapidly changing hog industry is the scene for the fourth case study. The Southeast Iowa Citizens for Community Improvement are fighting the large "factory farms" which have put in jeopardy a whole way of life and raise serious issues of air and water pollution.

Our fifth case study concerns the Anti-Displacement Project in Springfield, Massachusetts. This case describes the successful efforts of poor people to buy out and rehabilitate five large public housing projects and to establish and control a number of new economic initiatives which combine wealth and assets to benefit their communities and ensure long-term, decent-paying jobs for low-income residents.

The final case, *Comunidad en Movimiento*, is a parish-based community activity of Dolores Mission, one of the poorest parishes in Los Angeles. A group of Mexican women has stood up to the violence in their neighborhood and worked for peace establishing a safe-streets program and community policing model project.

As will become evident each project was very different and at different stages of development. Some groups were very experienced, others more recently organized. Some were clearly successful, others struggling. Some were very closely related to parishes and congregations, others were not. However, all adhered to the CCHD's criteria and all were enlivened by themes of Catholic Social Teaching listed above—clearly some more consciously than others. After spending time with each community, a number of themes emerged and cut across all the cases. Human dignity and respect were always mentioned first. Women, young people, and new immigrants were key actors. Training for community leadership and for jobs was a priority for every group. The need to "demystify the economy" kept emerging in discussions as well as the need for something akin to a "spirituality of work." Affordable housing, health insurance, and childcare were on everybody's mind. The need for transparency in government and business allowing for meaningful dialogue with workers was another focal issue. In addition, concern for the environment is rapidly gaining a voice among the working poor.

Three characteristics stood out. First, the involved community organizations held religiously to the view that there are no permanent enemies. While strong stances might be called for, alliances and partnerships, whether with government or business, were always sought. Second, participants in the cases were in it for the long haul. The poor understood that quick fixes don't work. They are committed to the long struggle. Third, in each of the projects examined, I was struck by the subtle traces of Christ's paschal mystery. Repeatedly, groups faced apparent failure, even death—but they did not give up. They somehow were able to elicit new options out of those apparent failures. They were able to turn death to resurrection.

The issue of faith-based organizing demands further elaboration. Churches have played a key role in providing space for discussion across racial and ethnic lines. Although not all of our cases are examples of faith-based organizing, all are, in some ways, influenced by this approach. CCHD's faith-based organizing goes back to the 1970s. But in the last few years, the organizing role of churches, synagogues, and increasingly mosques, has moved to the national stage. Political scientist Meredith Ramsey has highlighted the importance of faith-based organizing as well as the need for non-threatening "free spaces" for learning and discussion. "Where do ordinary people, steeped in lifelong experiences of humiliation, barred from acquisition of basic skills of citizenship—from running meetings to speaking in public—gain the courage, the self-confidence, and above all the hope to take action on their own behalf? . . . For Americans, particularly black and Hispanic Americans, that free space is most often found in church" (Meredith Ramsey, "Redeeming the City: Exploring the Relationship between Church and Metropolis," *Urban Affairs Review* 33 [May 1998]: 618–619).

METHOD

In each of the cases the author loosely followed the method known as the "pastoral circle." The approach has four basic steps. The first is *immersion* into the community or situation. Listen to the people, hear their story. What is going on? What are people feeling? Try to see what they are seeing. The basis for any understanding or analysis is lived experience. The second step in the circle is an *analysis* of the situation. What are the patterns? What are the important political, social, and economic factors? Who has the power? As Massaro reminds us, "humility before the data" is important. Only then can we really understand the issues. In the third step we reflect on our understanding of the issues. That *reflection* is based on our faith perspective, scripture, Catholic Social Teaching, and our grasp of the working of the Holy Spirit in the community. With this faith reflection we can now make a judgment on the issues. The fourth step in this pastoral circle concerns *decision* and *action*. Given the experience—now analyzed and reflected on—what should one do? If we have enough information, we move to action.

This is, in a nutshell, the method which I followed and would suggest might be a helpful approach for the individual reader or discussion group. Listen to the story, experience with the people, understand the issues, make a judgment based on faith as to where you stand on the issue, and then act on your judgment. You will obviously note how the people have acted and then whether the case prompts you to some action. For many individuals and parish groups, two reactions often arise when one reaches the action stage. The first is that situations of poverty and injustice are too complicated. There is always the other side of the story or more to learn. The second reaction is the nagging sense that one person, one committee, or one parish is powerless before such a huge problem. Don't be put off. Both concerns are paralyzers!! Acting alone is difficult but a community, parish, or diocese acting together can accomplish a great deal. Read the cases, reflect on what the six struggling organizations have accomplished. That in itself will be an incentive to action.

The method, outlined above, closely parallels CCHD's "Journey to Justice" process retreat which attempts to prayerfully assist participants to recognize the struggles of those who are poor and to help break down the myths and stereotypes about poverty in the U.S.A. The journey consists of three phrases—planning, a weekend immersion retreat with leaders from a CCHD project, and follow-up action.

One further point deserves mention before moving on to the case studies themselves. Frederick Perella, one of the formulators of CCHD's education for justice approach, recently praised the Campaign's early accomplishments. He also mentioned some shortcomings. One in particular caught my attention. Perella pointed out that although projects involved clergy and laity, they rarely involved the parish faith community as such.

The initial event of the Journey to Justice process is a weekend retreat that is designed for twenty to twenty-five participants. This retreat consists of eight sessions that build on each other and represent a key part of the total conversion process. During the retreat, participants are led through reflection on and discussion of the scriptural call to justice and Catholic social teaching, especially as they relate to the preferential option for and with the poor. A major and key portion of the second day of the retreat is devoted to a lengthy immersion experience with a CCHD funded group (or other empowered low-income group as defined by CCHD and Catholic Charities USA). Following the immersion experience, participants are introduced to the concept of social sin and its relation to personal sin. This is followed by a session on social analysis within the context of the pastoral circle. The participants are then called to imagine anew what can be done to address root causes of poverty in their community. The final session is a call to commit to taking the first step to make real their image of a just community by agreeing to attend a post-retreat meeting. This is often done within the context of a liturgy. (Ulrich, *Parish Social Ministry*, p. 104.)

"Such projects therefore were not often seen as expressions of evangelism or development of the community of faith. Overt effort to integrate prayer and spiritual reflection into the dynamics of the projects has been rare" (Frederick Perella, Jr., "Roman Catholic Approach to Urban Ministry, 1945–85," in Clifford J. Green, ed., *Churches, Cities and Human Community: Urban Ministry in the United States, 1945–1985* [Grand Rapids, MI: Eerdmans, 1996], p. 204).

CCHD funding, of course, is open to all, regardless of faith commitment or church affiliation. Many groups with no religious ties are funded. Nonetheless, the author saw a notable change from Perella's earlier observation. This change likely, but not entirely, relates to the increase in faith-based organizing. Scripture reflection, public prayer, ecumenical services, sacramental vision, and liturgy all emerged in the context of the work described below—obviously in some cases more than others. Moreover, the parishes and congregations involved in the projects reviewed show a direct link, a continuum, between charity and justice and between personal sin and social or structural sin. They sought consciously to relate faith and justice. In a few instances, as we will see, there is explicit linkage of social justice concerns to Catholic Trinitarian theology and Eucharistic liturgy. Some of what I saw and heard was captured by the provocative questions of urban faith-based organizer, Clifford J. Green:

> Ministry to cities needs . . . a renewal of faith vigorous enough to meet the challenge of the urban context. Will biblical faith be revised so that it is as hopeful of public redemption as personal salvation, of social justice as of peace of mind? Will a new and enduring practice of lay vocation in public life arise? . . . Will a new ecumenism be born to serve the new millennium? The formidable challenge of renewing American cities exposes the equally formidable task of renewing the American Churches. *Veni Creator Spiritus!*" ("Seeking Community in the Metropolis: Reflections on the Future," in Green, ed., *Churches, Cities and Human Community*, p. 307.)

Indeed, *Veni Creator Spiritus*—Come Holy Spirit. The reader will find much of the Spirit and the new ecumenism that Green calls for in the following case studies. Moreover, it is often the faith connection that keeps communities going, sometimes in the face of a violent "culture of death." In the Gospel of John 1:38–39, Jesus issues an invitation to "come and see." You are invited to do just that—come along on the CCHD journey to justice and get to know some of your American neighbors. You will see many credible signs of Christ alive and meet many Good Samaritans— most of them poor people but also many priests, ministers, sisters, politicians, business people, and parishioners like you.

DISCUSSION QUESTIONS

1. Discuss the parable of the Good Samaritan. What might be some applications for you today?
2. Talk about the biblical roots of justice. How do you see scripture influencing your views of justice and politics? Why do you think Jesus might be understood as the justice of God?
3. Read through the seven themes of Catholic Social Teaching. Try to apply these themes to some current situations in your own parish, city, or region.
4. Discuss the meaning of solidarity between the poor and non-poor. Can you think of any current examples?
5. Talk about the four steps in the pastoral circle: immersion-experience; analysis-understanding; reflection-judgment; action-decision. Discuss each step with your group. Why is this method described in a circle?
6. Discuss your understanding of CCHD and its approach to helping poor people become empowered. How has your parish or diocese been involved with CCHD?

OPTIONAL FURTHER STUDY

Catholic Campaign for Human Development, *Empowerment and Hope: 25 Years of Turning Lives Around* (Washington, DC: USCCB, 1986, being revised).

Catholic Campaign for Human Development, *Principles, Prophecy, and a Pastoral Response: An Overview of Modern Catholic Social Teaching* (Washington, DC: USCCB, 2001, rev. ed.).

Furfey, Paul Hanly, *Love and the Urban Ghetto* (Maryknoll: Orbis Press, 1978).

Green, Clifford J., ed., *Churches, Cities and Human Community: Urban Ministry in the United States, 1945–1985* (Grand Rapids, MI: Eerdmans, 1996).

Henriot, Peter J., Edward P. DeBerri, Michael J. Schultheis, *Catholic Social Teaching: Our Best Kept Secret* (New York and Washington, DC: Orbis Books/Center of Concern, 1992).

Holland, Joe, and Peter Henriot, S.J., *Social Analysis: Linking Faith and Justice* (New York and Washington, DC: Orbis Books/Center of Concerns, 1983, rev. ed.).

Kammer, Fred, S.J., *Doing Faithjustice: An Introduction to Catholic Social Thought* (New York: Paulist Press, 1991).

Kavanaugh John, and Mev Puleo, *Faces of Poverty, Faces of Christ* (Maryknoll: Orbis Books, 1991).

Massaro, Thomas, S.J., *Living Justice: Catholic Social Teaching in Action* (Franklin, WI: Sheed and Ward, 2000).

McKenna, Kevin E., *A Concise Guide to Catholic Social Teaching* (Notre Dame, IN: Ave Maria Press, 2002).

Melchin, Kenneth R., *Living with Other People: An Introduction to Christian Ethics Based on Bernard Lonergan* (Collegeville, MN: Liturgical Press, 1998).

Stoutzenberger, Joseph, *The Christian Call to Justice and Peace* (Winona, MN: St. Mary's Press, 1987).

Ulrich, Tom, *Parish Social Ministry: Strategies for Success* (Notre Dame, IN: Ave Maria Press, 2001).

USCC, *In All Things Charity: A Pastoral Challenge for the New Millennium* (Washington, DC: USCC, 1999).

USCCB, *Sharing Catholic Teaching: Challenges and Directions—Reflections of the U.S. Catholic Bishops* (Washington, DC: USCC, 1998).

Windley-Daoust, Jerry, et al, *Living Justice and Peace: Catholic Social Teaching in Practice* (Winona, MN: St. Mary's Press, 2001).

1

+

Grace Over Chicken: The Delmarva Poultry Justice Alliance

Pocomoke City, Maryland

SETTING: THE REAL COST OF DINNER

The American promise of a "chicken in every pot" takes on new meaning today. Chicken consumption has skyrocketed in the U.S. It is considered both healthy and inexpensive. Per capita consumption of chicken surpassed that of beef for the first time in 1992. Perdue and Tyson have become household names. They get both the praise and the profit from our Sunday dinner and backyard barbecue. But who really brings these tasty meals to our tables? And at what cost? A recent pastoral letter signed by 41 Catholic Bishops entitled *Voices and Choices: A Pastoral Message on Justice in the Workplace from the Catholic Bishops of the South* describes the suffering of poultry workers which "exacts an intolerable personal and community cost." Maria, for example, is careful to say how glad she is to be employed but after five years on a poultry processing line her fingers, hands, wrists, and back ache. She suffers pain, numbness, and disability from her repetitive motion job. "The pain often keeps her awake at night . . ." Maria is part of the poultry industry's "disposable workforce."

A large chunk of the poultry industry is concentrated on the Delmarva Peninsula, the eastern shore of the Chesapeake Bay, comprising Delaware and parts of Maryland and Virginia. The bay area is fabled for its natural environment, beaches, seafood, and chicken. Delmarva, though relatively small in size, is the fifth largest poultry production area in the U.S. Sussex County, Delaware, for instance, ranks first in broilers in the country, producing more than 200 million chickens per year. Approximately 17,000 people on Delmarva are involved in the industry which produces three billion pounds of chicken a year, raised on over two thousand five hundred farms and processed in eleven plants. But the rapid growth and shift from small family farm to a corporate assembly line industry have taken a devastating toll on workers and their families, small farm owners, and the environment.

In 1994, Father Jim Lewis, an Episcopal priest, was sent by his Bishop to Delmarva to try to forge an alliance of people and organizations who live and work around the poultry industry. As a result of unfair labor practices and concern for the environment, small farmers, workers, and environmental groups joined hands with faith communities—Baptists, Catholics, Episcopalians, and Methodists—to form an alliance. Through the efforts of those groups, with leadership from Father Lewis and Carole Morison, one of the small farmers, the Delmarva Poultry Justice Alliance (DPJA) was launched in 1996.

The Catholic Bishops' words raced through my head as I drove around Delmarva among the low-slung but sprawling chicken houses. During the 1990s, the large corporations involved in poultry had netted gigantic profits. According to the U.S. Department of Agriculture, the value of poultry production from 1987 to 1997 had doubled. The National Interfaith Committee for Worker Justice indicates that broiler industry operating profits exceeded one billion dollars in 1996. Why then were so many workers and small farmers suffering in the midst of this booming industry? Like most Americans, I had no idea of the story behind my favorite meal. During a visit to the DPJA, I found out by meeting many people just like Maria.

Poultry workers, young and old, men and women, stopped by the storefront office in Pocomoke City, Maryland. They told their stories with a disarming honesty that was, at once, gentle and brutal. Gentle because the overall goal in their organizing effort was clearly based on giving and gaining respect and dignity. But brutal because the fear which hovers about the industry was apparent in their description of the hardships and indignities imposed upon them. I was meeting with the foot soldiers of the poultry industry. I was confronted by all the fingerprints on the chicken. I was confronted by the first principle of Catholic Social Teaching (CST), that the human person is a reflection of God and possesses a basic dignity that comes from God and not from race, gender, or income. I was listening to chicken catchers, small farmers, and plant workers, and I was confronted by the grace I say before meals. Bless us, O Lord, and these Your gifts . . . but at what cost?

Herb, a fifty-year-old catcher with a bright smile, said his doctor told him that his bald head looked like a road map because of all the scars re-

> The dignity of the human person is a transcendent value, always recognized as such by those who sincerely search for the truth. . . . Every person, created in the image and likeness of God and therefore radically oriented towards the creator, is constantly in relationship with those possessed of the same dignity. To promote the good of the individual is thus to serve the common good, which is that point where rights and duties converge and reinforce one another. (John Paul II, *1999 World Day for Peace Message*, no. 2.)

sulting from twenty-six years of hitting it on low rafters in the dark chicken houses. This, of course, got a laugh from his co-workers. But more seriously he reported how he suffers from headaches and dizziness from the feathers, dust, ammonia, and 95-degree temperatures in the catching areas. George, who is in his late sixties, described his twelve years of work in the industry which left him with severe allergies, no health insurance, and a retirement check that is drawing him into poverty. Will and Sheila, a young couple both employed in a poultry processing plant, sadly recounted the accident that almost cost Will the use of his right hand because of a faulty, poorly maintained industry elevator. Will, like most of the workers, did not know his worker's compensation and medical rights. He was eventually fired for going to his own doctor rather than the company medic. Sheila described the eight to twelve hours on the plant assembly line standing in deep puddles of icy water, mud, and chicken feces while enduring the repetitive motion task of cleaning, cutting, or packaging chickens which race by on the conveyor belt. Simple amenities such as bathroom breaks were very sparse or lacking. A study by the Public Justice Center highlighted the dangers of stringent rules concerning bathroom breaks. "The negative effects of these stringent rules proved even more detrimental to pregnant women. Most shockingly . . . rules reportedly led workers to relieve themselves while working on the line . . ."

> The ultimate injustice is for a person or group to be treated actively or abandoned passively as if they were nonmembers of the human race. (U.S. Catholic Bishops, *Economic Justice for All*, 1986, no. 77.)

Patrick, a former chicken catcher, described how working conditions motivated him to lead the court challenge on behalf of catchers against Tyson Foods. Patrick now devotes his energies to organizing with DPJA. John, a seventy-two year old, described in detail the plight of the small farmer who is caught in a cycle of high investment and low profit. While the large corporations have experienced a profit margin of 15 to 30 percent, the small farmer realizes a profit of only 1 to 4 percent. In 1995, according to a Louisiana Tech survey, on average, annual profits for small chicken growers nationwide was $12,000 and shrinking. Carole Morison stated, "Big companies exploit small family farmers." She and her husband invested over $200,000 to build two 500 foot-long chicken houses. In addition, Perdue Farms' policy required the installation of a $15,000 drinking system for the chickens and a $30,000 building to store chicken manure to avoid polluting run-off. The debts keep mounting. The small farmers, "growers" as they are called, are afraid to protest the contract arrangement because they are mortgaged to the hilt.

> The structure of the present-day situation is deeply marked by many conflicts caused by humans and the technological means produced by human work play a primary role in it. . . . In view of this situation we must first of all recall a principle that has always been taught by the Church: the principle of the priority of labor over capital. (Pope John Paul II, *On Human Work*, 1981, no. 12.)

Here is how the process works. Five times a year, Perdue delivers 54,400 day-old chicks to the Morisons. The chicks are raised for seven weeks. The Morisons pay for all costs—feed, antibiotics, and disinfectants—all supplied by Perdue. At the end of the seven weeks, Perdue pays the Morisons about 18 cents per five-pound broiler. The chickens are owned by Perdue, the manure and pollutants are owned by the Morisons. This injustice is perpetrated by the unfair, one-sided contract arrangement. Carole Morison, who now directs the DPJA says, "We are all caught in the cycle. It's a kind of indentured servitude. This is a David and Goliath situation and the poultry alliance has given us a voice to help level the playing field."

> In this matter, the principle laid down . . . in the encyclical letter *Quadragesimo Anno* should be borne in mind: "It is totally false to ascribe to a single factor of production what is in fact produced by joint activity; and it is completely unjust for one factor to arrogate to itself what is produced, ignoring what has been contributed by the other factors." (Pope John XXIII, *Christianity and Social Progress*, 1961, no. 76.)

From hatchery to supermarket, the poultry business is what is called a "vertically integrated" industry. A single company controls production, processing, and distribution of the product. Each step in the process is tightly woven together in a pyramid that feeds profits upwards to the controlling company. Although profits and business links are "integrated," the levels in the pyramid are segregated off from one another. Chicken catchers who are mainly male and African-American, plant workers who are increasingly female and Latin, and small farmers, mainly white, have worked in isolation from one another and often in jealous competition. "Vertical integration" has promoted "horizontal segregation" and from a management perspective negates the Catholic principle of subsidiarity.

Just as it is gravely wrong to take from individuals what they can accomplish from their own initiative and industry and give it to the community, so also it is an injustice and at the same time a grave evil and disturbance of right order to assign to a greater and higher association what lesser and subordinate organizations can do. For every social activity ought of its very nature to furnish help (*subsidium*) to the members of the social body and never destroy and absorb them. (Pope Pius XI, *The Reconstruction of the Social Order*, 1931, no. 79.)

In the past, tension among white farmers, black catchers, and Latino plant workers has been divisive and destructive. While these communities have traditionally been divided, the DPJA has worked hard at bringing them together, promoting trust and mutual respect, and trying to build up some modicum of local control in the industry, thereby embodying Catholic Social Teaching's principles of solidarity and subsidiarity.

Historically, these communities would not even have known each other or known about the common injustice they suffer. Workers would not have spoken up for fear of losing their jobs and growers were silent for fear of losing their farms. But DPJA provided the space at the table for open discussion, and the Catholic Campaign for Human Development supported this faith-based organizing effort because of its potential for long-term positive change.

. . . [W]ork which [people] share together causes them to have common hopes, sorrows, desires, and joys, unites their wills, their minds, and hearts. For when [people] work they recognize one another as [brothers and sisters]. (Pope Paul VI, *The Development of Peoples*, 1967, no. 27.)

The problems in the industry are enormous from both a human and environmental perspective. In 1999, seven deaths of Tyson workers around the country were reported within five months, including a fifteen-year-old Mexican boy electrocuted by a faulty fan while catching chickens on a company-contracted farm. The DPJA rallied workers in front of the Tyson plant in Berlin, Maryland, to protest the unsafe working conditions and the need for job training (Chris Guy, "Coalition Holds Rally at Tyson Plant . . .," *Baltimore Sun*, October 28, 1999, and AP, "Group Asks for Probe of Tyson," *Wilmington News Journal*, October 29, 1999). As the Bishops' Pastoral Letter points out, "According to OSHA, health and safety violations involving a 'substantial probability of death or serious injury' increased more than 150% between 1997 and 1998 at one of the leading poultry processing companies."

Environmental degradation is another by-product of the rapid, forced-feeding, assembly-line mode of raising chickens. When chickens live, they belong to the company; when they die, they belong to the farmer. Farmers are responsible for disposing of the carcasses as well as the disastrous effects of the polluting manure run-off. Rivers have become polluted and large numbers of fish have been killed, reportedly by the disease phisteria. The small poultry farmers are left with the blame. Father Lewis exposes the lie in that misplaced blame. "In reality, poultry companies are responsible for the manure since the birds are owned by the company." Profits flow up to the large companies. Pollution flows down to small farmers and local communities.

> Indiscriminate application of "advances in science and technology . . . has led to the painful realization that we cannot interfere in one area of the ecosystem without paying attention both to the consequences of such interference in other areas and to the well-being of future generations." (Pope John Paul II, *The Ecological Crisis: A Common Responsibility*, no. 6.)

THE DISPOSABLE WORKFORCE

The Public Justice Center named its study of the Delmarva poultry industry *The Disposable Workforce*. Indeed, the vertically integrated poultry industry seems to consider its workforce, along with the small farmers and the environment, "disposable." Workers' rights and the right to organize for the chicken catchers and poultry plant workers have been the primary focus of the DPJA.

Patrick and Charles described for me the almost unbelievable job of chicken catcher. Their bleak tale came home to me as I ducked my head into a hot, dusty chicken house and was amazed to see 25,000 baby chicks scatter in a cloud leaving behind hundreds of tiny, lifeless carcasses— dead—usually from infection caused by a reaction to vaccinations. The job of catcher is dirty and dangerous. Arms and hands are bruised, scratched, and infected.

The work of the catcher is really the stuff of a Dickens novel. "Eleven o'clock at night, eight men stand in the dark parking lot of a local shopping mall. A company truck arrives, driven by the crew chief, to take the men to an unknown destination. The poultry company has arranged the catch with the farm—which might be ten miles away or fifty miles away." On arrival, the catchers pile out of the truck, unload the company equipment, and begin a night of work. The team is expected to catch—by hand—55,000 five-pound chickens ready for slaughter. The men do not get paid for travel or set-up time. Pay begins only when they start catching chickens. Systematically catching four or five chickens in each hand, catchers shove and stuff them into cages. Zooming in and out in the dark dust, a company forklift picks up the cages and loads them on trucks. Exhaust, dust, and ammonia hang heavy in the dark air so thick that one cannot see from one end of the chicken house to the other. They wear no protective gear and suffer cuts and bruises as well as chronic respiratory illnesses.

Patrick explained that the work day, or night, often lasts for twelve to fourteen hours depending on the availability of company trucks. Each worker is paid on the basis of the number of live chickens he catches— about $2.50 for every thousand chickens that arrive at the plant. As one catcher put it, "I have to catch about 2,000 chickens to afford to buy one at the supermarket!" The Catholic Bishops tell us, "A study of Delmarva chicken catchers shows that average daily compensation has declined since 1985. Additionally, over 60 percent of plants surveyed by the U.S. Department of Labor in 1997 fail to pay overtime to chicken-catching crews for hours worked over 40 per week" (*Voices and Choices*, p. 3).

Until recently, catchers were not considered employees of the poultry company but rather independent contractors without overtime, health insurance, or retirement benefits. With the ongoing assistance of DPJA and the Public Justice Center, lawsuits were filed, and won, for the right to be considered regular employees of Perdue and Tyson with full benefits as well as back pay for overtime. The catchers have continued their organizing effort and have affiliated with the United Food and Commercial Workers International Union.

In spite of these obvious important legal victories that hold promise for the catchers, Charles surprised me with his final remark. In response to

> People have the right to decent and productive work, to decent and fair wages, to private property and economic initiative. Workers have the strong support of the Church in forming and joining union and worker associations of their choosing in the exercise of their dignity and rights. (U.S. Catholic Bishops, *A Century of Social Teaching*, 1991, p. 6.)

my question as to how DPJA impacted his life and his family, he quietly replied that he feels better talking to his children, now that the catchers had stood up for themselves. Also he said, "with the new pay and retirement benefits, I will have something to leave them when I die. That makes me feel like a father."

Sheila, Will, and later Gustavo described in detail the conditions under which plant workers function. Their description echoed the Public Justice Center report, "Hanging on hooks, birds whiz by on the processing line at a rate of 50 to 90 per minute." Workers struggle to keep repeating the same movements over and over for a whole shift. As one author put it, "only inhuman hands could withstand the pain caused by as many as 40,000 daily repetitions of a single defined movement . . . set by a relentless conveyor belt and reinforced by circulating foremen. . . ." Many plant workers suffer from repetitive motion disorders in their hands, wrists, arms, and necks, and carpal tunnel syndrome. Wet and slippery floors, knife cuts, and burned eyes from the acidic spray of gall bladders are some of the usual disablers of women on the assembly line. Very little training and few safety procedures are offered for workers using high-tech and dangerous equipment. Bathroom breaks, as noted above, are severely limited—because slow down of the line decreases productivity. Productivity and worker discipline are enforced by the issuance of "occurrence" notices, a kind of demerit system.

In spite of the demanding fast-paced work, plant workers have traditionally remained below the government-defined poverty level. According to the Department of Health and Human Services and Department of Labor statistics, although poultry production rose by approximately 100 percent in the 1990s, processing workers' wages remained static and were 60 percent less than the average wage for manufacturing workers. Since the majority of poultry plant workers are Latino immigrants, organizing for better wages and working conditions is delicate and demanding. Gustavo, a DPJA organizer, works with Pilar Gomez, a representative of the United Food and Commercial Workers International Union, Local 27 of Georgetown, Delaware. They have struggled to assist immigrants from Guatemala, Honduras, and Mexico understand their rights and seek assistance. It is a difficult battle because of the fear factor. Workers are afraid.

Gustavo explained that companies recruit workers at border crossings and through an informal network because, lacking English, they are docile and will accept working conditions that U.S. citizens will not. Companies pay a per-head fee to finders. Some immigrants are legal; many are not. That, of course, opens the way to substandard pay, horrible working and living conditions, and the clear possibility of violating workers' rights with impunity. Pilar indicated that because the recruit-immigrants are afraid, a fear compounded if they are undocumented, organizing must be done in a culturally sensitive way. The DPJA and UFCW are committed to this task.

Faith communities are important support groups in this effort. Sister Maria, a Spanish nun who works with *La Esperanza* (Hope), a community service organization that assists the immigrant community, especially women and families, recounts one of her early encounters with the poultry industry and Father Lewis's efforts. It was at a rally in support of workers after one of them lost a finger in a processing plant. The Central American workers were fearful of speaking out but when they recognized the nuns in the first row of the protest, they stood their ground. Sister Maria understands well the fear and intimidation the immigrants suffer. She likened the poultry workers to the Israelites in Egypt: their work is grueling but they put up with it with a kind of docile loyalty. They don't complain out of fear of deportation.

> Made in the image and likeness of God, newcomers remind us that most Catholics in the United States are descendants of those who arrived here to begin a new life. Different in look, customs and language, newcomers are often discriminated against. It is not a new situation in the journey of many centuries. "You shall also love the stranger, for you were strangers in the land of Egypt . . ." (Dt 10:19).
>
> These brothers and sisters face many challenges in common, including questions of a living wage, and other workers' rights, human dignity and immigration issues. These brothers and sisters, made in God's image and likeness appear to have no choice in their employment situation. (*Voices and Choices: A Pastoral Message on Justice in the Workplace from the Catholic Bishops of the South*, pp. 3–4.)

The concerns of Gustavo, Pilar, and Sister Maria were confirmed in December 2001, when a federal grand jury indicted Tyson Foods executives on charges of conspiring to smuggle illegal immigrants into the U.S. to work in poultry plants. The indictment stated that the company cultivated "a corporate culture in which the hiring of illegal alien workers" was condoned by management "to meet its production goals and cut its costs to maximize Tyson profits" (*Washington Post*, December 20, 2001).

As the legal and union victories of the catchers become better known, plant workers are becoming more interested in learning their rights, seeking support and empowering their own community. The DPJA and the UFCW provide that opportunity. Hope is in the air and the wider public, especially faith communities, are being challenged to hear the pleas and help. Indeed as Father Lewis indicated, respect, dignity, and solidarity—principal themes of Catholic Social Teaching—are discussed in everyday language around the DPJA table. "It is a real Pentecostal event to sit at a Delmarva Poultry Justice Alliance meeting and see Latinos, African-Americans, white farmers, union members . . . newly arrived Guatemalans, third generation 'locals,' environmentalists, and bird lovers talking and working around common issues. . . ."

ACTIVITIES AND ACCOMPLISHMENTS

The Delmarva Poultry Justice Alliance has succeeded in making the injustices of the poultry industry known to a wide audience through coverage by CBS' *Sixty Minutes, Iowa Public Television,* and *The New York Times.* Accomplishments include:

- With the support of the Public Justice Center, filed and won a lawsuit on behalf of Perdue catchers in 1998. The federal judge called Perdue "unfair and negligent" in its treatment of workers. Perdue catchers voted for union representation.
- In June 1999, Tyson catchers, with the volunteer assistance of Baltimore attorney C. Christopher Brown, sued for recognition as company employees and for back overtime pay. The judge ruled in favor of the workers, and a fair settlement was reached in November 2001.
- On May 10, 2002, and August 8, 2002, the *Washington Post* reported that Perdue Farms had settled with the Labor Department to pay $10 million in back wages for employee time spent putting on and taking off protective gear needed for work. The Labor Department also filed suit against Tyson Foods when agreement could not be reached in a similar case.
- Secured Maryland Department of Labor's investigation of the death of a Tyson worker. Tyson was cited for serious safety violations and ordered to improve worker safety.
- Worked closely with local, state, and federal government agencies as well as members of Congress to strengthen enforcement power

where violations of agriculture, meatpacking, and livestock laws and regulations are uncovered.

- Participated in the Maryland Environmental Legislative Summit to expose the unlawful pollution of land and rivers. Contributed to nationwide efforts to rid chicken feed of antibiotics and other additives.

EVALUATION/IMPACT

Building on human dignity, trust, and solidarity, the Delmarva Poultry Justice Alliance with the support of the Catholic Campaign for Human Development has built a coalition of poultry workers, churches, union, and environmental and animal rights organizations. Upon his arrival in Delmarva, Father Lewis realized that the "Church must not only address the daily pastoral problems of people . . . but also the justice issues that lie at the heart of the economic and social problems of the people served."

The efforts of DPJA directly affect about 17,000 poultry workers on Delmarva and indirectly well over 100,000 people who are dependent on the industry. Moreover, the model of organizing and supporting growers and workers has been replicated in other parts of the country. Poultry alliances have been formed in Georgia and North Carolina, and the alliance idea is being studied for application to other agricultural and livestock businesses.

REFLECTION

When we reflect on the plight of poultry workers, we realize that our grace before meals is being shouted back at us by the voices of the poor. Catholic concern for justice travels down to us through the Old Testament prophets and Jesus' identification with the poor and vulnerable. We are called to "action on behalf of justice." When we listen to the stories of the growers, catchers, and plant workers, the principles of Catholic Social Teaching take on flesh and bones. We need not be put off by complicated concepts such as "vertical integration." No concept can justify fear, inhuman working conditions, poor wages, and environmental degradation. The Delmarva Poultry Justice Alliance is a clear case where people of faith are realizing they can cut through the complexities and jargon and be supportive of organizational and reform efforts. The DPJA does not seek the demise of the poultry industry. On the contrary, the growers and workers want to see it flourish but with greater concern for ethics, equity, and environment. There need to be greater safeguards for small farmers, workers and their families, and the environment. The racially and culturally diverse partnership that the DPJA has forged should be a lesson and challenge to all of us as we accept and act on the call to solidarity with the poor which is such a focal issue for John Paul II.

When Father Lewis started his work in Delmarva, some likened his approach, usually sarcastically, to the prophets. Indeed, he often sounded like the prophet Amos who lashed out against those who cheated and exploited the poor in order to maximize profit:

> Hear this, you who trample upon the needy
>   and destroy the poor of the land!
> "When will the new moon be over," you ask,
>   "that we may sell our grain . . .
> We will . . . add to the shekel,
>   and fix our scales for cheating!" (Am 8:4–5).

While Lewis would agree with Amos, he was also calling all of us who pray grace over our chicken dinner to examine the issues and forge alliances to do away with the injustice. His approach and that of the DPJA mirror the teachings of modern Catholic Social Teaching—human dignity, solidarity with the poor, rights of workers, and concern for the environment. Father Lewis reminds us, "Christianity is about love, but justice is love with its work clothes on!"

In *Voices and Choices,* our Bishops engage in a conversation with all the partners in the poultry industry but call us to identify with the problems of the workers: "Why are their problems our problems?" The pastoral letter is a call to Catholics and other faith communities to take the "next step" to support reform in the poultry industry. "Lord when did we see you?" Do we see the image of the divine in the face of those who work in the poultry industry and other such businesses? As Catholic Christians, what are we called to do?

Food and meals are a focal point of the Catholic sacramental vision. Jesus was constantly inviting people, all kinds of people, to dinner parties or picnics. Right before He died, He shared a meal with His closest followers (Mt 26:26–28). That meal—the Eucharist—constitutes the central act of Catholic worship. For Catholics, the family dinner points to the Eucharist and as *The Catechism of the Catholic Church* reminds us, the Eucharist "commits us to the poor" (#1397). That is part, at least, of what "grace" before meals is about.

Bless us, O Lord—our grace has been disturbed, and it ought to be! As Wendell Berry, poet and environmentalist, reminds us, "What's the use in thanking God for food that has come at an unbearable expense to the world and other people? Every eater has a responsibility to find out where food comes from and what its real costs are, and then to do something to reduce the costs." *Amen!*

DISCUSSION QUESTIONS

1. How does your job compare to the chicken catchers and poultry plant workers? Do you know anyone with such grueling work?
2. What does Catholic Social Teaching mean when it claims that labor should take priority over capital? What do you think about that?
3. As a group, discuss what needs to be done to reform the poultry industry? What might you or your parish do to contribute? Would you be willing to pay more for the chicken you buy?
4. Discuss what you really know and think about unions. Do you know anyone in a union? Why did they join? Why do the poultry workers join?
5. Discuss how Catholic Social Teaching principles compare/conflict with "vertical integration" in business.
6. How might the plight of poultry workers affect the way you pray grace before meals?

SUGGESTED PARISH ACTION

Contact the DPJA for a copy of the CBS *60 Minutes* program or to obtain other videos on the poultry industry. View as a group and discuss for possible action steps.

CONTACTS

Delmarva Poultry Justice Alliance
145A Market Street
Pocomoke City, MD 21851
Tel. 410-957-9699, 877-460-8423

OPTIONAL FURTHER STUDY

William Bole, "Poultry Justice," *Commonweal* CXXIX (October 25, 2002) pp. 10–11.
Chesapeake Bay Foundation and Delmarva Poultry Justice Alliance, *Bay Friendly Chicken: Reinventing the Delmarva Poultry Industry*, December 2000.
Thomas Massaro, *Living Justice: Catholic Social Teaching in Action* (Franklin, WI: Sheed and Ward, 2000), pp. 119–124; pp. 138–142.

Public Justice Center, *The Disposable Workforce: A Worker's Perspective* (Baltimore: PJC, 2000).

Voices and Choices: A Pastoral Message on Justice in the Workplace from the Catholic Bishops of the South; Voces y Opiciones: Una Carta Pastoral de los Obispros Catolicos del Sur (Cincinnati: St. Anthony Press, 2000).

2

✛

The Living Wage:
Tenants' and Workers'
Support Committee

Alexandria, Virginia

SETTING: A LIVING WAGE AND BUDGET WISELY

Being poor is tough and humiliating anywhere, but it is even more painful being poor in a well-off area. That is a part at least of the suffering of the working poor of Northern Virginia. "Old Town Alexandria" with its cobblestone streets and colonial setting on the banks of the Potomac is a magnetic tourist attraction. Ringed by classy hotels, fine restaurants, and trendy taverns, the historic district is a must-see area for tourists, convention attendees, and local visitors. Visitors, however, usually see but don't pay much attention to the multiracial and multiethnic workforce. Nestled not far from Old Town is a narrow strip of Central America—Arlandria-Chirilagua—a neighborhood wedged in one mile south of National Airport and part of Alexandria. The community is home to about 12,000 low-income Latinos and African-Americans with a mixture of African and Asian immigrants. While the Alexandria area boasts a median family income of about $80,000, most of its large working poor scrape by with minimum wage jobs. Alexandria is a microcosm of the rich-poor divide in the U.S.; it has the highest per capita income in Northern Virginia but also the highest concentration of low-income minority peoples. In spite of an elevated income rate, the city has one of the highest youth poverty levels in the area.

The Tenants' and Workers' Support Committee (TWSC), a community-based organization, grew out of a 1986 effort of local residents to prevent the eviction of 5,000 low-income people from their homes. The TWSC has expanded to become Northern Virginia's only multi-issue and multiracial

grassroots organization focusing on the concerns of low-wage working people, especially women. The Catholic Campaign for Human Development
has helped to fund this initiative in organizing, leadership development,
and coalition-building. Parishes, congregations, and synagogues have
pulled together to support TWSC's defense of the poor—especially in the
fight for the city of Alexandria's living wage law.

The living wage is not an abstraction but rather represents a fair standard of what a family needs and what Catholic Social Teaching principles endorse. Sometimes referred to as a "just wage" or a "family wage,"
it encompasses much more than our current notion of a minimum wage.
Think about the question, what does it mean "to earn a living." Some of
us make many times over what we need to live very comfortably. Some
of us scrape by from paycheck to paycheck. But we all have a gut sense
of how much it takes for a family "to live." A living wage means that
payment for work should be adequate so that a man or woman can support themselves and their families with modest dignity and some security for the future. In Catholic Social Teaching, that includes a decent
salary relative to the local cost of living, access to health care, benefits
such as vacation and personal days, and some savings for the future.
In some areas, a living wage has been calculated at one dollar above
the minimum wage, but, in most areas of the United States, a living
wage has been estimated to be about double the minimum wage. It
should be noted that, either way, it still results in a very low salary. In
addition to the living wage campaign, TWSC has organized its efforts
around health and medical insurance, childcare services, education,
and housing.

> Let it be granted, then, that, as a rule, workman and employer
> should make free agreements, and in particular should freely agree
> as to wages; nevertheless, there is a dictate of nature more imperious
> and more ancient than any bargain between man and man, that the
> remuneration must be enough to support the wage earner in rea-
> sonable and frugal comfort. If through necessity or fear of a worse
> evil, the workman accepts harder conditions because an employer
> or contractor will give him no better, he is the victim of force and in-
> justice. (Pope Leo XIII, *On the Condition of Labor,* 1891, no. 45.)

In many ways, TWSC and its director Jon Liss serve as the community's
court of last resort—where to go when all else fails; but more importantly,
as a prod to the community to help itself. TWSC clarifies issues, nurtures
and trains young leaders, and tries to empower the next generation. These

local leaders, in turn, work to organize the community and influence policy and legislation.

TWSC is located in the heart of Arlandria and is a bustling hub of activity. Mt. Vernon Avenue, the main drag of Arlandria, has a series of Salvadoran, Guatemalan, and African shops. Music and the aroma of fresh *empanadas, tamales, pupusas,* and *kolo* fill the air. St. Rita's, a predominantly Latino parish, is the local landmark. The area is poor and run-down, but like most immigrant neighborhoods, it is bursting with energy and a veritable field of dreams about new beginnings, family, education, and jobs. TWSC provides a kind of hotline for worker abuse, dangerous working conditions, racial and sexual harassment, and intimidation of workers who support unionization. The evening I visited TWSC, it was filled with high school students helping to transport senior citizens to polling stations for the Virginia election.

> Do not grow slack in zeal, be fervent in spirit, serve the Lord. Rejoice in hope, endure in affliction, persevere in prayer. Contribute to the needs of the holy ones, exercise hospitality (Rom 12:11–13).

Cameron Barron, a staffer at TWSC, walked me through cavernous city-contracted parking garages to track down some of the workers who first-hand had participated in the living wage campaign. The two Ethiopian-born attendants I met happily recounted how the new living wage law literally changed their lives. Makonen Hastemarian said that at age sixty-eight he is delighted to have to work only one job as a parking lot attendant. He explained that this came after many years of working two full-time jobs. Finally, he has time to spend with his wife and two daughters. "Sometimes I go to theater or a concert. These things give some meaning to life." Makonen is a dignified man who was a teacher in his native Ethiopia. When he started working in the U.S., it was at the minimum wage; he had no choice but to work two full-time jobs to support his family. Another parking attendant described his *three* jobs, eight hours at the garage, eight hours in a 7-Eleven store, and a part-time job at a local pharmacy.

The passage of the living wage law provided a piece, at least, of the immigrants' dream come true. After a three-year effort led by TWSC, the Alexandrian City Council voted unanimously for a living wage to be paid to all city contract workers. Parking lot attendants in city-owned garages went from the minimum wage of $5.15 per hour to $9.84 per hour and were subsequently raised to over $10.00 per hour. The bright smiles on their faces betray a deep sense of relief and accomplishment as well as a new-found appreciation of the American democratic dream. Mr. Hastemarian readily admitted that for younger workers there was still a long steep road ahead. For many of the workers with families, the raise resulting from the living wage law means now they only have to work *two* full-time jobs!

Nonetheless, although modest in scope, the living wage law was a significant victory and the result of a broad coalition of concerned people. In one of the first meetings of the campaign, Father John McBrearty, SSJ, Pastor of St. Joseph's in Old Town, helped to mobilize support and was quick to relate the living wage to Catholic Social Teaching. To a packed interfaith service he said, "It is fitting for Catholics to [speak] out for jobs with justice. . . . Our own Catholic Social Teaching since 1891 down to the present Holy Father John Paul II and all his bishops have always addressed economic justice and the principle of human dignity." He quoted the United Nations Declaration of Human Rights, "Everyone has the right to just and favorable remuneration." That night, December 10, 1998, Father McBrearty did not endear himself to the Alexandria city fathers. Neither did Maria Cabrera of St. Rita's. "Our workers receive unjust salaries which force long hours and multiple jobs." "The struggle," she said, "leaves no time for family or rest." Rabbi Jack Moline added the voice of the Jewish prophets, "Countless times in the Torah we are reminded not to mistreat the worker, not to exploit the laborer, not to oppress the poor. . . . Servitude does not mean working without compensation. It means working without *adequate* compensation, without the wherewithal to provide for the needs of one's self and one's family."

> From this premise of the sacredness of human work, Catholic social teaching contributes a moral voice to such issues of economic justice as wages, working conditions, relations between employees and employers, the rights of workers to form unions and professional associations, and the duty of workers to develop their skills. Such questions are integral to the overarching concern about "economic arrangements that leave large numbers of people impoverished" (U.S. Catholic Bishops, *Economic Justice for All,* 1986, no. 74). (CCHD, *Principles, Prophecy, and a Pastoral Response,* 2001, p. 22.)

In January 1999, Rev. Daniel Brown of the Third Baptist Church and Rev. Roberto Morales of San Jose Episcopal Church led over 400 people to Alexandria City Hall. More than thirty leaders of local religious congregations, unions, and community groups signed a petition asking the city council to pass the living wage law. Sue Capers of the Virginia Coalition for the Homeless drove home the broader meaning of the living wage. "When we surveyed homeless shelters in Virginia, we found that

40 percent of these people were working . . . homelessness is too often caused by low wages, and a living wage law would help move people into self-sufficiency." Too often we view the homeless as mentally disturbed, drug- or alcohol-addicted, or simply too lazy to work. The reality in Northern Virginia, however, is that many are working hard at minimum wage jobs and unable to afford rent. The council got the message and unanimously voted in the law.

In a similar vein, Father Gerry Creedon, pastor of St. Charles Borromeo and a strong advocate for the immigrant communities, placed the living wage issue in the wider perspective of recent welfare to work reforms. "The whole idea of the new welfare law," he said, " was that once people get a job they can save and get out of poverty." Creedon said this was not happening to his African-American, Latino, and Vietnamese parishioners. Those helped by the new living wage law were faring better but most others were stuck in minimum wage jobs which keep them below the already artificially low federal official poverty level of $18,100 per year for a family of four. He added that the local community was hit hard by the economic downturn in the aftermath of September 11. It is estimated that 12,000 workers in the hotel and restaurant fields have been laid off in the greater Washington area. Father Creedon likened the campaign to the Irish struggle for inclusion in American society. He described some of the maneuvering that went on to build contacts and coalitions in support of the ordinance, as well as the strong opposition at the state level. It was a long tedious process involving numerous factions, but the effort was well worth it. He called the living wage victory a symbolic breakthrough for the working poor and a concrete expression of the Church's commitment to solidarity with the poor.

> The Church in America must incarnate in her pastoral initiatives the solidarity of the universal church toward the poor and the outcast of every kind. Her attitude needs to be one of assistance, promotion, liberation, and fraternal openness. The goal of the church is to ensure that no one is marginalized. (Pope John Paul II, *Ecclesia in America*, 1999, no. 58.)

THE HARDWORKING POOR

Amalia was one of the first people I met at TWSC. She is clearly one of the "senior citizens" of the organization, a long-time volunteer and currently board president. In many ways, Amalia, like other women from St. Rita's,

St. Charles', St. Joseph's, San Jose Episcopal, and Third Baptist are the "spirit" of TWSC—the "Marys" who work behind the scene. She described the changes in her community since she came from war-torn El Salvador. "In those days there was so much hope and promise." She remembers clearly her dreams of family, schools, and jobs. In spite of her poor circumstances, she is profoundly grateful for her life in America and the opportunities she has had. While hope still glistens in her eyes, she is concerned that the problems of jobs, health, and housing have worsened for immigrants and have taken a heavy toll on the young. They still arrive full of hope and dreams, but Amalia sees an increased number of young people, men and women, sleeping in the outside stairwells of her apartment complex as well as signs of drugs and gangs. She recounted that even though many times she was afraid, she hesitated to call the police because she knew the homeless had no where to go. But she was also strong—another "Mary" sign—in her defense of the young men who wait on Four Mile Run, a local thoroughfare, from 4 to 6 in the morning hoping to land temporary jobs as day laborers or painters.

At a time in her life when she has fewer responsibilities and could finally rest, Amalia pushes on in support of TWSC's efforts. For me, she beautifully embodied the lesson of the widow's mite. "Amen, I say to you, this poor widow put in more than all the other contributors to the treasury. For they have all contributed from their surplus wealth, but she, from her poverty, has contributed all she had, her whole livelihood" (Mk 12: 43–44). In a telling plea that speaks volumes, she referred to her community as the "hardworking poor." She said all of us had to understand what was going on. *"La gente esta dormida"*—The people are asleep; they need to wake up. Amalia meant both communities—the haves and have-nots, ours and hers. Her comments resonate through the Catholic experience and all the way back to Exodus: "You shall not oppress an alien; you well know how it feels to be an alien, since you were once aliens yourselves in the land of Egypt" (Ex 23:9). Indeed, some people have been awakened, and TWSC sounded the Virginia wake-up call!

TWSC's commitment to the community is expanding. Their Unity Project is an effort to organize childcare providers in Northern Virginia. Denise Wilkins, project coordinator for Unity, points out that while much lip service is paid to the need for good, safe and educational childcare, providers are usually on the bottom of the heap when it comes to salary and benefits. Denise is currently involved in a door-to-door campaign to organize and support city-contracted childcare providers. She introduced me to Allie, a contractor caring for seven to nine children from needy families. Her day begins at 4:00 A.M. and ends at 6:00 P.M. Her home is neatly laid-out with classroom, lunchroom, and outside playground. Allie is genuinely committed to the parents and children she serves. She provides wholesome meals, daycare, and a safe after-school environment but without any work benefits because of her "contract" status. The burning issue for her, of course, is health insurance.

> Besides wages, various social wages intended to ensure the life and health of workers and their families play a part here. The expenses involved in health care, especially in the case of accidents at work, demand that medical assistance should be easily available for workers and that as far as possible it should be cheap or even free of charge. (Pope John Paul II, *On Human Work*, 1981, no. 19.)

I asked Allie what impact, if any, TWSC's Unity Project has had on her. She hesitated a long while and thought about the question and then surprised me with her response. "In one word, *respect*," she said. "The city had no respect for the work we do and we were competing with one another. In this area, there has always been competition and not much trust. We were divided. When I went to my first Unity meeting, I was shocked but overjoyed at how people of all colors and national groups got along. There was warmth, love and, most of all, respect. Unity showed us another way; we don't get angry anymore, we get the job done." Allie, in her own quiet but determined way, captures well TWSC's approach to empowering local people to understand and fight for the issues that effect their lives.

> [W]ith respect to the fundamental rights of the person, every type of discrimination whether social or cultural, whether based on sex, race, color, social condition, language, or religion, is to be overcome and eradicated as contrary to God's intent. (Vatican II, *Church in the Modern World*, 1965, no. 29.)

Denise explained that Allie's reference to her first meeting concerned the city's unilaterally changing the dates caregivers received their checks. The notice letter from the childcare agency began, "Please budget wisely" while the agency changes the way it processes invoices. Low pay and late checks left little room for wise budgeting! Rent, utility, and car payments were late, credit card bills mounted and checks inevitably bounced. Some women received eviction notices. For many of us, one late check would not spell disaster, but for those who must make a little go a long way, a late check can start a disastrous chain of events. The TWSC fought back and Project Unity was born. Denise, Allie, and the other city-contract childcare providers argue now that the priority issue is health insurance. This uphill battle is now the primary focus of their efforts.

Silvia Portillo coordinates the "Healthy Community Project" for the committee. Silvia is a nurse from El Salvador and has experienced firsthand the sense of fear and abandonment families must face without medical insurance. Over 80 percent of the Hispanic adults in the area have no coverage. Moreover, in spite of steady work at minimum pay jobs, most have no understanding or receive any orientation about mandatory workers' compensation coverage. Most of the people who come through TWSC's door pay out of pocket for medical costs, including costs for work-related injuries and illnesses. That would be a horrendous expense even for middle-income families. Silvia indicated that language problems and culture issues are often disturbing and humiliating for new immigrants. Many members of TWSC rely on their children as translators and most have no understanding of our complicated system of medical access, insurance, and treatment. A common ear infection in a child quickly becomes a major crisis.

> Love of preference for the poor, and the decisions which it inspires in us, cannot but embrace the immense multitudes of the hungry, the needy, the homeless, those without medical care, and, above all, those without hope of a better future. (Pope John Paul II, *On Social Concern*, 1987, no. 42.)

To respond to such crises, TWSC under Silvia's leadership has begun an ambitious program in community health. Health fairs are held at churches and community centers and bring to the neighborhood volunteer doctors and nurses as well as medical screening and testing, preventive health practices, and medical referral services. In addition, a volunteer community health promoter course is offered for local women. Regular health classes are held, especially for pregnant women and young mothers. Fathers, too, are instructed in family care issues. Special sessions are offered and translation services provided for people needing access to medical and hospital care. A recent survey indicates that many residents who need serious medical treatment simply do not know what questions to ask or cannot ask them in English. Many leave the hospital with debts ranging from hundreds of dollars to over $30,000. This kind of debt obviously has a devastating impact on an immigrant family dependent on minimum wage jobs and leaves them vulnerable to predatory loan schemes. Through a concerted advocacy effort the TWSC Healthy Community Project has been able to get many of the debts dismissed or reduced.

Silvia, true to her nurse's role, says, "Questions about your health or a family member's health or your ability to pay for health services are always sensitive and often threatening; imagine what it is like to go to a hospital without English and without insurance?" Imagine!

ACTIVITIES AND ACCOMPLISHMENTS

Since 1986, TWSC has promoted human dignity and solidarity among arguably one of the most diverse population areas in the United States. Northern Virginia is not only diverse racially, culturally, and religiously, but also, and in extremes, economically. In its organizing efforts, TWSC has made a fundamental option to work with the poor and vulnerable and is committed to fostering leadership from within the community. It is expanding its operations to respond on a broader regional basis to issues of education, health, housing, and citizenship.

Accomplishments over the last five years include:

- Establishment of the Arlandria-Chirilagua Housing Cooperative with 282 resident-owned units
- Passed the first living wage ordinance in Virginia in June 2000
- Mounted three successful union campaigns for low-income immigrant workers resulting in over $1 million in wage, benefits, and health and safety improvements
- Brokered $2 million in relocation payments and rent subsidies for low-income families displaced by development in Arlington in 1999
- Secured $200,000 in community recreation facility improvements
- Organized health fairs for hundreds of families and trained 30 community health promoters
- Helped create a model dual-language elementary school program and make public schools more accountable to parents and local communities
- Initiated a program for documentation and eventual citizenship, especially for younger residents

EVALUATION/IMPACT

TWSC has provided a variety of services and support to the low-income community of Northern Virginia but the Committee, true to the Catholic Campaign for Human Development's philosophy, early on grasped the need to move beyond assistance to organization and empowerment, to build upon their direct service efforts to include social justice.

The living wage ordinance, although modest in numbers and limited to City of Alexandria contract workers, was a significant accomplishment. It involved a broad Northern Virginia coalition aligned with the nationwide movement which has been successful in a number of cities and counties around the U.S. The living wage and benefits for the lowest paid workers have also become issues on university campuses.

TWSC has 300 dues-paying members and over 250 outside supporters and donors. The institutional changes effected by the committee directly benefit 15,000 to 20,000 people and youth. Perhaps most importantly, organizing and leadership training, skills in participatory research, power and issues analysis, planning, and public speaking are being passed on to a new generation of leaders.

REFLECTION

Anyone who has ever tried to learn a new language will understand something of the anguish the new immigrant goes through. Adults experience themselves as children and are often so treated by others. Try to imagine for a moment what being poor does to that already intimidating situation. Immigrants come to our country just as most of our ancestors did to escape poverty and oppression. Like us, they dream of a job, a decent home, and the capacity to support a family. Unfortunately, too often, what they encounter is poverty and prejudice. The American dream becomes a nightmare. But it need not be so as TWSC and numerous faith communities in Northern Virginia are proving.

> When an alien resides with you in your land, do not molest him . . . have the same love for him as for yourself; for you too were once aliens in the land of Egypt. I, the LORD, am your God (Lv 19:33–34).

Immigrant communities are the stuff of American Catholicism. It was not long ago that Amalia, Makonen, and Silvia might have been our parents or grandparents—not from El Salvador, Guatemala, or Ethiopia—but maybe Italy, Germany, Ireland, or Poland. The geography has shifted but the problems are the same—jobs, health, and housing. The Church stood with those earlier immigrants and is now calling us to stand by the new ones. This is the thrust of John Paul II, asking us all to walk "the path to solidarity." "Taking the Gospel as its starting point, a culture of solidarity needs to be promoted as capable of inspiring timely initiatives in support of the poor and the outcast, especially refugees forced to leave their villages and lands in order to flee violence" (*Ecclesia in America,* no. 25).

The family is the fundamental unit for Catholics. Our model begins with a poor family forced to flee into a powerful country. The familiar parallels are all too obvious, a young, brand new mother, a working-class father, and no affordable housing, so they "budgeted wisely" and "wrapped him in swaddling clothes and laid him in a manger" (Lk 2:7). We all know the story by heart but probably consider it too farfetched or too "holy" to apply today. But Silvia and Amalia see the same story reenacted every day.

Building support for the living wage for working families places us on the "path to solidarity with the poor" to which John Paul calls us. Such support is a concrete manifestation of the Church's "preferential option for the poor." Wages are only one link in the economic chain. Obviously for a business to be successful it needs to make a profit. But if maximization of profit comes by squeezing workers, there is injustice. For example, the ratio of compensation between the lowest paid worker and the highest paid CEO speaks volumes about a society's or a company's ethics. However, glaring differences in compensation between lower level employees and upper level executives have grown dramatically in recent years. In 1960, a CEO's salary in the U.S. was about twelve times that of the average factory worker; by 1995, it was about 135 times the average worker's salary. In 1997 *Business Week* reported that the ration was 326 to one! And that gap has continued to widen. This is one "sign of the times" which demands Christian reflection.

> Moreover, in the economically developed countries, it frequently happens that great, or sometimes very great, remuneration is had for the performance of some task of lesser importance or doubtful utility. Meanwhile, the diligent and profitable work that whole classes of decent and hard-working citizens perform, receives too low a payment and one insufficient for the necessities of life. . . . Wherefore, we judge it to be our duty to reaffirm once again that just as remuneration for work cannot be left entirely to unregulated competition, neither may it be decided arbitrarily at the will of the more powerful. (Pope John XXIII, *Christianity and Social Progress*, 1961, nos. 70–71.)

Matthew's parable of the laborers in the vineyard (Mt 20:1–16) which has perplexed people since its telling might be of help in our reflection. Frankly, most of us are probably turned off by this story, even offended and irritated that the latecomer is paid the same as the guy who worked all day. To be sure, the deeper meaning of the story has to do with the Jewish covenant and the place of Gentiles in God's plan of salvation. The parable is about God's generosity to all of humanity, but, for our purposes here, it also manifests a very earthy and humane understanding of the horrible working conditions of day laborers at the time of Jesus. Men searching for casual labor jobs hung around the "agora," a kind of public market place, hoping to be hired by landowners. The "denarius" represented something like the living wage—enough to get by on. We catch a glimpse of an alternative vision of what the world could be, what God's promised kingdom is about, from the landowner's generosity. One denarius is the bare minimum—what a worker needs—no matter how long he works—in order to "earn a living." Again, the story is lived out today. Every morning workers wait in "agoras" across America. In Northern Virginia, the "agora" happens to be called Four Mile Run.

Fair treatment of workers has always been a "jewel in the crown" of Catholic Social Teaching. In 1891, Pope Leo XIII lit the torch for a "just wage" by rejecting an "iron law" that determined salaries strictly on the basis of supply and demand, cost-cutting, and markets. That flame ignited vibrant support in the U.S. Church that began with Msgr. John A. Ryan's 1906 classic *A Living Wage.* Nonetheless, as we have seen, the same wage debates continue today. The principle has been passed on through Pius XI, John XXIII, Paul VI, and John Paul II, and continues to energize American Catholic Social Teaching. In 1986, the Bishops of the United States reminded us that, "The most urgent priority for domestic economic policy is the creation of new jobs with adequate pay and decent working conditions" (*Economic Justice for All,* 1986, no. 136).

As we reflect on the work of TWSC, we gain a different perspective on issues most of us take for granted: a decent job with wages and benefits adequate for our family, a roof overhead, and health coverage. To a great extent, these have come to define the American dream. On the other hand, as we listen to TWSC members hopefully we also have gained a better understanding of what the Church teaches about human dignity, family, solidarity, the option for the poor, and the rights of workers. We should be clear that a living wage does not mean that the housemaid will be paid the same as the executive, or the receptionist the same as the doctor, but it does mean that the employer-employee relationship is one of mutual respect and dignity. And that respect and dignity should be reflected in the paycheck. It also means that we recognize our need for the Amalias and Allies of this world.

> The key problem of social ethics . . . is that of just remuneration for work done. In the context of the present there is no more important way for securing a just relationship between the worker and the employer than that constituted by remuneration for work. (Pope John Paul II, *On Human Work,* 1981, no. 19.)

Although the teaching is clear and the principles intact, the flame is being buffeted by strong economic, political, and global winds. Application is the test of principles. In a very real sense, we, like the new immigrants, need to learn a new language and apply it if we are to recognize Jesus in the poor. The words of our Holy Father test the language and call us to reflective action: ". . . a just wage is the concrete means of verifying the justice of the whole socioeconomic system . . . of checking that it is functioning justly" (*On Human Work*, 1981, no. 19).

DISCUSSION QUESTIONS

1. Do you know anyone trying to raise a family with a minimum wage job? What do you think that is like?
2. Could you and your family get by without health insurance? How would you handle it?
3. Can our economy afford the living wage? Can you? How might a living wage for lower level workers affect you and your neighbors?
4. What do you think when you hear of homeless people or people on welfare? Has your thinking changed in light of the living wage issue?
5. How do social and economic conditions in our country square with gospel values?
6. Why do you think Catholic Social Teaching is so strong in its advocacy of the living wage?
7. What can you personally or your parish do to welcome and support immigrants?

SUGGESTED PARISH ACTION

Invite a speaker from a living wage group and discuss how you might become involved and take action in this national movement. Organizations listed below can provide names of speakers in your area.

CONTACTS

Tenants' and Workers' Support Committee
P.O. Box 2327
Alexandria, VA 22301
703-684-5697

ACORN Living Wage Resource Center
739 8th Street, SW
Washington, DC 20003
202-547-2500
www.acorn.org

National Interfaith Committee for Worker Justice
1020 West Bryn Mawr, 4th Floor
Chicago, IL 60626
773-728-8400
www.nicwj.org

OPTIONAL FURTHER STUDY

Frank D. Almade, "Just Wage," in Judith A. Dwyer, ed., *The New Dictionary of Catholic Social Thought* (Collegeville, MN: Liturgical Press, 1994), pp. 491–495.

Barbara Ehrenreich, *Nickel and Dimed: On (Not) Getting by in America* (New York: Metropolitan Books, 2001).

Patricia Ann Lamoureux, "Justice for Wage Earners," *Horizons* 28 (Fall 2001), pp. 211–236.

Thomas Massaro, *Living Justice: Catholic Social Teaching in Action* (Franklin, WI: Sheed and Ward, 2000), pp. 115–119; pp. 124–127; pp. 138–142.

Charles R. Morris, "The Living Wage," *Commonweal* CXXIX (October 11, 2002) pp. 9–10.

Katherine S. Newman, *No Shame in My Game: The Working Poor in the Inner City* (New York: Vintage Books, 2000).

3

Taking a City off the Cross: Camden Churches Organized for People

Camden, New Jersey

SETTING: CAMDEN, NEW JERSEY—THE WAY OF THE CROSS

The City of Camden, New Jersey, is usually described as the "second poorest city in the country, located in the second richest state." But that might be damning with faint praise. Camden might be the worst-case scenario. What the visitor who wanders off 676 on the way into Philadelphia experiences is miles of potholed streets, the stench of raw sewage, abandoned homes, numerous outdoor drug markets, and ubiquitous broken glass. The reaction is, in most cases, fear and then anger, especially for the human toll—the collateral damage from company closings, white and middle class flight, and incompetent and corrupt local government. The anger is almost irrepressible, especially when one thinks of Camden's children.

Indeed as New Jersey hovers at or near the top of our most affluent states, Camden has plummeted to being possibly the poorest city in the nation. Per capital income is under $10,000. More than 57 percent of Camden's children live in poverty—three times higher than the state's average.

The crushing poverty has created a public health crisis for children. The infant mortality rate (2.4 percent) is almost four times higher than the rest of the state and twice the rate found in some developing countries. On average, a Camden infant dies at the rate of nearly one a week. Kids are exposed to a very high level of violence. In spite of recent improvement in public safety, the city is the sixth most violent place in the United States.

Indeed, Camden is a city of children, and the effect of this poverty on them is deep and disturbing. More than 38 percent of residents are younger than nineteen, but only 51 percent graduate from high school. Statistically, individuals without high school diplomas are likely to have lifetime incomes below the poverty level. This means that one out of two children in Camden can expect to live in poverty for the rest of his or her life!

Camden also has the highest number of vacant and abandoned houses in New Jersey and perhaps the highest in the country. Picture a street where one out of every five houses is boarded up; that is what Camden looks like. The city has only one full-service grocery store for 80,000 people!

How in God's name could we let this happen in one of the most affluent areas in the United States? How could we so victimize a city of 80,000 people, 35,000 of them children? As a Camden priest put it, "They think a mother's heart can't break in Camden."

What the visitor to Camden might not see, however, is the human and Christian side of Camden—a hope-filled group of Church people who daily walk the way of the cross for their families and community. They call themselves Camden Churches Organized for People (CCOP). Ron Evans, a Korean War vet, is a former chairman of CCOP and an active member of St. Bartholomew Catholic Church. His whole adult life has been given to the struggle for a new Camden. After so many years, he is convinced "we can't put a Band-Aid on cancer. . . . In Camden everything is broken. We need action now."

Rosa Ramirez, a long-time member of St. Joseph's Pro-Cathedral Parish and a CCOP activist, describes with great passion her dedication to organizing for a better Camden. She told me of one of the CCOP's early efforts involving a busy drug corner in her East Camden neighborhood. The abandoned building was the scene of assaults, rapes, and lucrative drug traffic. The site even served as a shooting gallery where young boys were trained in the use of handguns. The neighborhood was paralyzed with fear but eventually, with leadership from Rosa and others, sought help from St. Joe's and CCOP. Rosa described how Msgr. Robert McDermott, the pastor of St. Joe's and a Camden native, defied the drug lords with a liturgical procession that blessed the notorious corner asking for God's forgiveness and creative action in the Spirit. The community found strength from this public way of the cross and decided together to respond. Supported by the organizing skills of CCOP, the neighbors rallied, confronted the druggies, and motivated the police to take action. CCOP then worked with the St. Joseph's Carpenter Society, the parish's non-profit housing agency, to purchase and rehabilitate the abandoned property. Today that once death-filled corner of Camden houses a hard-working and community-minded family. Rosa said it was one of the first little steps in Camden's "stations of the cross" and it led to a resurrection—death overcome by new life.

Rosa's hope is for a city where children can grow and not be "prisoners" in their homes, where going to school does not mean walking by abandoned houses, drug dealers, prostitutes, and pimps. She said too many parents honestly feel they cannot let their children go outside. Rosa spoke of a co-worker at St. Joseph's School who had diligently saved up enough to buy her little boy a new bicycle. "She was so happy." But when Rosa inquired, "Where does he ride?" the mother responded, "In the basement."

Rachel mourns her children. . . .
Cease your cries of mourning,
    wipe the tears from your eyes. . . .
There is hope for your future, says the LORD;
    your sons shall return to their own borders (Jer 31:15–17).

Early one morning before the workday began, I met with Rev. Heyward Wiggins and his wife Gloria. Rev. Wiggins is pastor of Camden Bible Tabernacle and the current chair of CCOP. A Camden native with a biblical faith that surrounds his every word and movement, Rev. Wiggins was catapulted into community leadership by a curious inner-city experience. When a store owner near his church proposed to open a seemingly innocent new business, a twenty-four-hour laundromat, neighbors became suspicious. Drug dealing was a big problem. Adding an all-night establishment promised another "hot spot" drug corner. Violent crime and prostitution were already on the rise. Moreover, twenty-four heavy duty washing machines working around the clock were sure to worsen the already weak and dirty water supply. What tilted Rev. Wiggins further into the need to organize and educate neighbors was the rude awakening at the zoning hearing when lawyers for the absentee business owner cross-examined local residents "like *we* were criminals." People who questioned the wisdom of a twenty-four-hour establishment in an already crime-ridden neighborhood out of concern for their children felt themselves threatened by local authorities. Neighbors were not asking for much: "They want to sit on their front porch without someone harassing them or sneaking in the back door. They want streets cleaned and the sewers fixed. They don't want big things. They want little things" (*New York Times*, July 12, 2000). Rev. Wiggins, along with his congregation began a deep personal and community journey on what is now called "faith-based organizing."

Juanita Cruz is another very active member of St. Joe's and a leader of the local organizing committee for CCOP. For so long she was afraid to speak up, but "CCOP taught us to be leaders and to speak out." She has learned to observe situations, analyze issues, find out who is responsible and has power, write down her thoughts, propose solutions, and take action. Juanita has had to struggle with learning English but now does not hesitate to stand up in meetings and demand responsibility from city, county, and state officials. It is beautiful to behold! CCOP has made her feel part of a team, a larger effort, where she can truly live out her Catholic faith and serve her community. For Juanita, *"union es fuerza"*—there is strength in unity. She is now deeply committed to recruiting and training other CCOP leaders and she drives a hard bargain. "If Jesus Christ would suffer and die for us, we should be willing to give a few hours to our suffering and dying community. CCOP is offering the only ray of hope." Reminiscent of the women who wept for Jesus on the way to Calvary, Juanita ended our conversation by saying that "Camden is worth crying for because eventually our crying will be tears of hope and joy."

> As he drew near, he saw the city and wept over it, saying, "If this day you only knew what makes for peace—but now it is hidden from your eyes" (Lk 19:41–42).

The CCOP represents thirty faith-based institutions and over 10,000 people. They are people truly walking a way of the cross with their city. The Catholic Campaign for Human Development supports the community organization because it saw promise in its faith-based organizing and the strong commitment of local leaders to the long haul of social change in the city. *USA Today,* July 27, 2000, summed up CCOP's journey: "[Camden is] a place where the government cannot collect its taxes, board up its derelict buildings or enforce its housing code, where hope must fight like a weed through the cracked pavement. All that holds this city together is a network of churches, community groups, and non-profit agencies, plus residents too stubborn or poor to leave." The journalist got most of it right—he should have added or "too faith-filled" to leave.

THE WORST-CASE SCENARIO

In spite of some signs of hope and inherent advantages such as proximity to Philadelphia and shipping port facilities, Camden lacks two key ingredients for an economically healthy city—businesses and middle-income residents. A CCOP leader puts it bluntly, "Camden can't be a warehouse for the poor and survive. We need a share of middle-income people who can make the city a better place to live."

However, Camden has lost that middle-income population. Suburban growth and exclusionary policies have made the city an "enclave of concentrated poverty." In a very real sense the city has become a scapegoat for the region, a "warehouse for poor minorities."

Public safety is a major concern, especially for Camden's young people. Homicide is the leading cause of death for fifteen- to twenty-five-year-olds. Camden's nine square miles are home to over 150 drug markets. The drug business is one of the city's leading employers. Although over 50 percent of drug buyers come from outside the city, the drug traffic has victimized local people. Youngsters are recruited as "scouts" or "trappers," respectively warning dealers about police presence or seeking out new customers.

An additional factor in Camden's demise, which sounds like the height of irony, is that the city is saddled with property tax rates that are substantially higher than their more affluent suburban neighbors and New Jersey as a whole. Nonetheless, in spite of high taxes, city government has not been able to serve its people. Many essential services are contracted out to county, state, non-profit, or church groups. Many businesses have left Camden frustrated by the miles of red tape and the muck of corruption. Three of the city's last five mayors have been indicted and convicted on serious criminal charges. The mistrust of elected officials is deep.

CCOP: ORGANIZING IN FAITH

In spite of this discouraging situation and the sheer weight of statistics, Camden's faithful have not lost hope. CCOP was formed in 1985 and is affiliated with the Pacific Institute for Community Organization (PICO), a faith-based national organization which offers training and technical assistance to help empower low-income families. In this model, congregations of all faiths serve as the basis for organizing communities. Core leaders from each church, like Ron, Rosa, Juanita, and Rev. Wiggins, meet with local residents and build a network around common issues.

The glue holding the network together is a faith-based commitment to seek the common good. Joe Fleming has been the dedicated lead organizer for CCOP for twelve years. His faith perspective motivates his actions, and his guiding principle is "Don't do for others what they can and should do for themselves." The training of local leaders is his priority.

Overall, it is the churches which have provided the most reliable leadership in Camden's struggle for the common good of families and neighborhoods. Like Jeremiah, the people still hope in God's promise for their city. "For it is I this day who have made you a fortified city, a pillar of iron, a wall of brass, against the whole land. . . . They will fight against you, but not prevail over you, for I am with you to deliver you, says the Lord" (Jer 1:18–19).

Desperate because of the lack of support from local government and frustrated by decades of unfulfilled promises from county, state, and federal agencies, local residents turned to the only credible institutions left in the city—the churches. The struggle—the way of the cross, the search for the common good of a dying community—became the unifying factors.

CCOP began literally with a big stink! When the county needed a regional sewage treatment plant where thirty-seven municipal centers could dump raw sewage, Camden, the most densely populated part of the county, got it. The people of the city were offered no remuneration and the stench was unbearable. Msgr. Michael Doyle, pastor of Sacred Heart, the parish in which the sewage plant is located, attributed the decision to "racism and great disrespect for the poor." It was clear Camden needed an organization which could unite different factions, help people understand the issues, and articulate an "option for the poor." CCOP was born. After a three-year struggle led by the church groups, a $3.2 million annual payment was won for city residents and businesses to offset the impact of the regional sewage treatment plant. A victory surely, but the stench remains!

> [I]t is the poor and the powerless who most directly bear the burden of current environmental carelessness. Their lands and neighborhoods are more likely to be polluted or to host toxic waste dumps, their water to be undrinkable, their children to be harmed. Too often, the structure of sacrifice involved in environmental remedies seems to exact a high price from the poor and from workers. (U.S. Catholic Bishops, *Renewing the Earth*, 1992, 2.)

By the mid nineties, virtually every street in Camden was dotted by rat-infested, vandalized, abandoned houses. Because of Camden's high property taxes, for many residents, unemployed or working for minimum wages, it was cheaper to walk out rather than try to sell a home. New "tenants" were often drug dealers, hookers, or arsonists. City officials couldn't even offer an estimate of the number of abandoned houses. According to the *Courier-Post* (June 2, 1996), estimates ranged from 2,000 to 5,000 with half of those properties city-owned through foreclosures. CCOP took up the challenge and mobilized over 1,000 people to survey and map the location of empty buildings. They enlisted the help of Rutgers University's Center for Social and Community Development and the Camden police and fire departments. They also sought the collaboration of the New Jersey Department of Community Affairs and local non-profit housing organizations such as St. Joseph's Carpenter Society. The mapped-out findings were presented to a large city meeting. Joe Fleming described the "audible gasps" from the audience as they finally were able to connect abandoned houses with higher crime and lower property values. The *Philadelphia Inquirer* (July 15, 2002) headline read, "Razing Abandoned Houses Cuts Crime. . . ." The initiative gathered momentum and resulted in the boarding-up of over 2,000 dangerous buildings and the demolition of 500 units. In its effort to build a city "worthy of its children," CCOP also took up other very sensitive city-wide issues, such as the need for more and safer recreational facilities for young people and the importance of more community involvement with the police department.

Faith-based community organizing as it has evolved in Camden provides a prime example of applying not only gospel values but also some of the major principles of Catholic Social Teaching—solidarity, participation, subsidiarity, and the common good.

Solidarity emphasizes the point that human beings depend on one another. In Camden that solidarity was built by CCOP's bringing church people together. Neighborhoods and congregations had to listen, understand, and prioritize what was best for the whole city. They had to move beyond narrow self-interest. Parishioners had to realize the importance of their personal and communal power and to channel that power to serve the common good. Most importantly, they had to understand and put into practice their own core principle "power is taken, not given." White, black, and Latino congregations, Catholic and Protestant, drew upon their biblical and liturgical roots to provide the framework for empowerment, responsible collective action, and servanthood.

> The exercise of solidarity within each society is valid when its members recognize one another as persons. . . . Positive signs in the contemporary world are the growing awareness of the solidarity of the poor among themselves, their efforts to support one another, and their public demonstrations on the social scene which, without recourse to violence, present their own needs and rights in the face of the inefficiency or corruption of the public authorities. By virtue of her own evangelical duty, the Church feels called to take her stand beside the poor, to discern the justice of their requests, and to help satisfy them, without losing sight of the good of groups in the context of the common good. (Pope John Paul II, *On Social Concern*, 1988, no. 39.)

Participation is fundamental to this process. Most people have and need some control over their lives and the ability to participate in the decisions that affect them and their families. For decades this has not been so in Camden. Sewage, prisons, property tax structures, drugs, and crime have overwhelmed the city like a blizzard. Residents have had no voice.

As Msgr. Doyle dramatically put it, "they at least should have the right to know the name of the boot on their necks!" Indeed, CCOP has given them the chance to participate and to understand the deeper structural questions, to put a name on the boot!

> The principle of participation leads us to the conviction that the most appropriate and fundamental solutions to poverty will be those that enable people to take control of their own lives. For poverty is not merely the lack of adequate financial resources. It entails a more profound kind of deprivation, a denial of full participation in the economic, social, and political life of society and an inability to influence decisions that affect one's life. It means being powerless in a way that assaults not only one's pocketbook but also one's fundamental human dignity. (U.S. Bishops, *Economic Justice for All*, 1986, no. 188.)

Subsidiarity is the key principle for understanding what has gone on in Camden and the role that CCOP plays, especially over the last year. Put simply, subsidiarity means that in normal circumstances, authority and power should be kept at the local level. Keep decision making closest to those most directly affected. It is a core principle of democracy which demands both citizen participation and competent and honest local political leadership. Participation and local control have been the hallmark demands of CCOP since its inception. However, as the organization soon realized, the grim reality was that local government was not equal to the task of dealing with Camden's problems.

> As history abundantly proves, it is true that on account of changed conditions many things which were done by small associations in former times cannot be done now save by large associations. Still, that most weighty principle, which cannot be set aside or changed, remains fixed and unshaken in social philosophy: Just as it is gravely wrong to take from individuals what they can accomplish by their own initiative and industry and give it to the community, so also it is an injustice and at the same time a grave evil and disturbance of right order to assign to a greater and higher association what lesser and subordinate organizations can do. For every social activity ought of its very nature to furnish help to the members of the body social, and never destroy and absorb them. (Pope Pius XI, *The Reconstruction of the Social Order*, 1931, no. 79.)

A NEW VISION FOR CAMDEN

By the beginning of 2000, it became apparent to CCOP, the churches, and the non-profits that they were being compelled to serve as a substitute government, doing the thinking, planning, and resource identification that any normal city government would be expected to do. CCOP was nursing a city on life support. It was also clear that the blight was now spreading to communities surrounding the city. The state of New Jersey was covering about 70 percent of the municipal budget. Funds were used almost exclusively to cover operating expenses—mainly police and fire services. Camden has not had a budget in which money is invested in infrastructure and capacity building in twenty years! Just keeping Camden on life support was costing the state about $65 million per year.

By April 2000, state officials began to question the high cost of "life support" and introduced the possibility of a state takeover of local government. Following on the heels of the indictment of Camden's mayor and another series of audits critical of the city government's financial management, the state started shopping for potential partners—state and county agencies, as well as non-profit organizations. CCOP and member organizations were acutely aware of the gravity of Camden's situation; rebirth would be impossible without significant outside intervention—both financial and human. However, they were also acutely aware of the hard-won civil rights issues and the importance of participation and local control. The principles of Catholic Social Teaching—participation, solidarity, and subsidiarity—remained operative. Rather than opt for a "takeover," CCOP, working in partnership with Concerned Black Clergy (CBC), chose a different, more positive course.

It was a thorny dilemma but a major step on Camden's way of the cross. CCOP leaders realized they could no longer shore up a dysfunctional and dishonest system that should have gone belly-up many years ago. Again true to their principles, the churches dug into the root causes of Camden's poverty. As a long-time pastor told me, "the people refused to die on their backs." CCOP, and their allies CBC, set to work and developed "A Vision for the Recovery of Camden." On June 13, 2000, with a massive turnout of over 1,200 people at St. Joseph's Pro-Cathedral, the plan was presented to state and local officials.

The vision is framed by the words of the Old Testament prophet Habakkuk which speaks volumes to Camden's frustratingly long wait made more painful by broken promises.

> Write down the vision
> Clearly upon the tablets,
> so that one can read it readily.

> For the vision still has its time,
>   presses on to fulfillment,
> and will not disappoint;
> If it delays, wait for it,
>   it will surely come, It will not be late (Hb 2:2–3).

After so long a wait and such struggle, the vision was widely discussed so all could see and hear the justice of it—and act upon it. The churches' proclamation envisioned ". . . a city in which children and families experience the fullness of God's creation. . . . The painful reality is that the needs of children and adults in the city have gone unmet for too long, on a scale unrivaled anywhere else in the state of New Jersey. The present governmental structure has wholly failed to modify or improve the outcome of our residents. Given the complexity and uniqueness of the situation, we believe a bold and creative alternative must be implemented."

Keeping the city on life support was a kind of slow and costly crucifixion. CCOP's "bold and creative" vision called for improved delivery of services to city residents in public safety, housing, social services, economic development, and education. The vision also demanded concrete action in two critical areas. The first was human capital. Camden needs a cadre of managers and elected officials who have the expertise and experience to effectively deliver services in the nation's poorest city. Leadership matters, CCOP said; too often corruption and incompetence had damaged the city's credibility and scared away potential public and private investment.

The second key factor the "Vision" addressed was the need for significant financial resources. Camden has a huge structural deficit that makes it impossible to meet the overwhelming needs of residents and businesses. Without a significant infusion of funds from the state and new policies that make development more attractive to public and private investors, there will be no recovery. Like a long-suffering hospital patient, Camden has been kept on life support, but denied the resources to achieve recovery.

> Also on the increase in America is the phenomenon of urbanization. . . . The frequent lack of planning in this process is a source of many evils. . . . "In certain cases, some urban areas are like islands where violence, juvenile delinquency, and an air of desperation flourish" . . . The evangelization of urban culture is a formidable challenge for the church. (Pope John Paul II, *Ecclesia in America,* 1999, no. 21.)

With "A Vision for the Recovery of Camden," CCOP took its faith-based organizing activity to a new and more ambitious level. While continuing work on discrete issues affecting everyday life, the church groups have broken through to attack structural and institutional problems that have mired the city in a "culture of death."

Msgr. McDermott articulated clearly what the "Vision" embodied. "We have challenged state officials to provide resources and expertise to the city, and we have challenged city officials to set aside bruised egos and find a workable way to partner with the state" (*Courier Post*, October 9, 2000). As pressure mounted, "takeover," at least in some quarters of the city, became a dirty word. But CCOP and CBC, sticking to their vision, stated their willingness to accept some form of state intervention but only if local people and local organizations were active participants in the recovery plan and implementation. Significant new resources, both financial and administrative were needed, but transition back to local control had to be integral to the plan. The Catholic principles of human dignity, participation, solidarity, and subsidiarity, and action on behalf of justice provided guidance. "If we are to create something new for the people of our city, especially our children, we need to move beyond the question: 'Who is to blame?' Instead, it is time to answer this question: 'What are we going to do about it?'"

By May 2000, the state had already assumed supervision of Camden's finances. But CCOP still did not want emphasis to fall on the "takeover." State intervention, necessary as it appeared to be, was only one part of the vision. Msgr. McDermott concluded, "The dignity and capacity of Camden residents to determine our destiny cannot be taken away or 'taken over.' There must be real participation on the part of the people of the city."

Toward the end of 2001, a Camden rescue plan almost made it. State senator Wayne Bryant picked up on the "Vision for Recovery" and proposed legislation that would infuse financial and administrative resources into Camden. The Bryant bill passed the State Senate but was shelved when New Jersey's new governor James McGreevy was faced with a $1.9 billion deficit. But Rev. James C. Jones and Rev. Heyward Wiggins, leaders of CBC and CCOP respectively, still spoke up for Camden's poor. They strongly objected to Senator Bryant's bill being shelved in tandem with support for a new sports complex in Newark. Both proposals were to be funded "later." But for the ministers, it was sacrilegious and fiscally shortsighted to equate sewage in the water system, boarded-up housing, and the cruel poverty of Camden with a sports complex. "It is morally indefensible to link a bill designed to improve basic conditions in the second poorest city in America with a project that would allow professional athletes in shorts to entertain wealthy patrons in a new and improved arena. The Camden bill should be passed on its own. It's the right thing to do"(*Courier-Post*, December 21, 2001).

The climb up Calvary continued. The people of Camden finally got their chance to meet face-to-face with Governor McGreevy. On March 7, 2002, 1,500 people packed Antioch Baptist Church in Camden's poorest neighborhood. CCOP and CBC patiently listened and understood the difficult position the governor was in—given the huge budget deficit he faced. However, CCOP's faith-filled witnessing, careful analysis, and supportive testimony from religious, political, and economic leaders from the whole surrounding area of South Jersey made resounding impact. The governor was clearly taken aback by the commitment and professionalism of Camden's core of Christian leaders. Rosa Ramirez challenged the governor, "Camden cannot wait any longer; our children need you to be a leader." Parents patiently told the governor that they feared for their children's lives—whether they would be harmed on the way to school. Carmen, fifteen years old, spoke for Camden's youth. She said she had learned in her young life not to trust politicians because "they always let us down." But she still pleaded with the governor to come to the aid of Camden's children. The governor now clearly was between the proverbial rock and a hard place but demurred, saying he did not want to make promises he could not deliver on. The people seemed to accept that as fair and forthright, but they were not prepared to let him off the hook.

A message from Camden's Catholic bishop Nicholas DiMarzio was read: "Most children in the city lack adequate education, health care, nutrition, safety—and hope. That reality challenges all of us to respond, especially those of us in positions of leadership." The bishop reinforced a focal argument of CCOP's presentation that in a very real sense all of South Jersey will benefit from a "healthier Camden." The blight was already spreading to the inner ring suburbs. South Jersey political leaders drove that point home.

The bishop's message continued, "We understand that you are dealing with a budget crisis. Camden's crisis runs much deeper, however, and requires immediate attention. The longer you wait to deliver a recovery package, the more it will cost the state. The longer you wait, the greater the number of children who will be lost to poverty, violence, and despair."

The March 7 meeting with New Jersey's new governor was a turning point for CCOP. On that night local people and local churches cut through to structures—they confronted structural sin.

The sum total of the negative factors working against a true awareness of the universal *common good,* and the need to further it, gives
the impression of creating, in persons and institutions, an obstacle
which is difficult to overcome. . . .

"Sin" and "structures of sin" are categories which are seldom applied
to the situation of the contemporary world. However, one cannot
easily gain a profound understanding of the reality that confronts us
unless we give a name to the root of the evils which afflict us. (Pope
John Paul II, *On Social Concern,* 1988, no. 36.)

Sean Closkey, director of St. Joseph's Carpenter Society, articulated the
CCOP's position and presented the governor with a stark choice: maintain the horrible status quo by keeping Camden on costly life support, *or*
move Camden toward recovery and self-sufficiency.

That historic night ended with yet another image from Camden's Stations of the Cross. Children carried in a dummy on life support and
placed the body in the sanctuary of the church. The governor dropped his
prepared response and promised to be back in Camden in sixty days with
a recovery plan for the city.

Governor McGreevy was true to his word and to Camden's kids. He
returned to Antioch Baptist Church on June 13, 2002, and presented his
plan for the recovery of the city. It was exactly two years to the day since
the CCOP had unveiled its "Vision" for Camden. The governor's plan
built on that vision as well as Senator Bryant's "Rehabilitation and Economic Recovery Bill." "Today we stand committed to addressing the
problems that, for too long, have stood in the way of Camden's progress
and economic growth. . . . This revitalization plan will take significant
steps toward restoring Camden's neighborhoods and economy." The
plan became legislation in Senator Bryant's bill and was quickly passed
by the state legislature. The bill calls for $175 million to be invested in
Camden's rehabilitation and includes: demolition of more than 1,000
abandoned buildings; rehabilitation of hundreds of residential units; repair of water and sewer systems; leveraging of private investments for
business revitalization and downtown development; enhanced public
safety and anti-drug efforts in collaboration with the state police; development of workforce training programs for Camden residents; and increased support for higher education institutions and hospitals. In addition, five new schools will be constructed, miles of streets re-paved, and
tax incentives offered to businesses willing to locate in the city. As for the

issue of human resources, the bill calls for the appointment of a chief operating officer to oversee city agencies and manage economic development. It also calls for more state control over the school board and public school operations. Two oversight boards were established which will include members of the local community appointed by the governor.

On July 22, 2002, in the presence of a large CCOP contingent, Governor McGreevy signed the Camden Recovery Bill. Habakkuk's vision resounded throughout the state house: "For the vision still has its time, presses on to fulfillment, and will not disappoint." What faith! What faith-based organizing! But still CCOP and CBC plan to keep vigilant. Rev. Floyd White said after the signing, "The Vision's there. With accountability and commitment, it will work." Msgr. McDermott added, "We need to make sure as an organization that all those resources really do affect the residents and get to all the neighborhoods. . . . If we could raise the standard of living for kids and other folks, that's a victory." And what a victory for CCOP and Camden!

ACTIVITIES AND ACCOMPLISHMENTS

CCOP brings together families and congregations from different racial, ethnic, and religious backgrounds in a common effort to address serious concerns in what is arguably the poorest city in America. Accomplishments include:

- Leveraged $3 million in new state funds to allow Camden non-profit organizations to develop over 120 units of new housing
- Boarded up over 2,000 abandoned buildings and demolished over 500 dangerous units
- Won $3.2 million annually for Camden residents to offset the impact of the regional sewage treatment plant
- Worked with county prosecutors and Camden police to eliminated open-air drug markets
- Developed "A Vision for the Recovery of Camden," which was incorporated into the Camden Rehabilitation and Economic Recovery Bill of 2002

EVALUATION/IMPACT

Camden Churches Organized for People represents thirty faith-based institutions and over 10,000 people. However, its impact goes well beyond its direct membership and touches virtually all of Camden's 80,000 residents. CCOP's organizing impact has gained support in surrounding counties and throughout South Jersey.

The Catholic Campaign for Human Development supports this effort in solidarity with the poor as well as its movement toward structural and institutional change. Working through local churches, the organizing effort focuses on strengthening relationships—one on one, family to family, and congregation to congregation. Local leaders grow out of local churches. *The Courier-Post* has recognized CCOP as the "largest and most effective community organization in the city."

REFLECTION

It should be no surprise that the traditional devotion of the Stations of the Cross has a significant role in Camden. Each station reenacts the ultimate preferential option for and with the poor. Jesus and his people have fallen under the weight of the cross more than three times. But thanks to a vibrant Church presence—committed laypeople, sisters, ministers, and priests—there are many Simons to help carry the cross and many Veronicas to wipe away sweat and tears.

> Sacred Scripture reminds us that God hears the cry of the poor (cf. Ps 34:7), and the church must heed the cry of those most in need. Hearing their voice, she must live with the poor and share their distress. By her lifestyle, her priorities, her words and her actions, she must testify that she is in communion and solidarity with them. (John Paul II, *Ecclesia in America*, 1999, no. 58.)

Camden has become known as one of urban America's worst-case scenarios, but the real story is Camden's people, the heart and soul of the community who have striven to build a city "worthy of its children." I was moved by the faith and hope in the midst of suffering that motivate Camden's churches. Carrying their city on life support, as Jesus carried the cross, Camden's faithful look hopefully to Resurrection. CCOP's "Vision" demanded a long patient Way of the Cross but it did not disappoint.

> For the vision still has its time . . .
> and will not disappoint;
> If it delays, wait for it,
> it will surely come, It will not be late (Hab 2:3).

The sad truth of many American inner cities is that the only functional institutions left are liquor stores, drug markets, and churches. Often churches remain the only credible and stable presence in low-income neighborhoods. For the really poor they provide the only "free space" for crossing racial, ethnic, and economic lines, for confronting problems and channeling despair into hope and constructive action. Usually it is the only space open to all. CCOP and its member churches have created that space for Camden. And it has done that by promoting the idea of being servants for the common good.

Each year in February, CCOP sponsors a "Christian Unity Week" and at the same time honors Martin Luther King Jr. The year 2002 was particularly important given all that was going on in the city. Msgr. Doyle was asked to offer a reflection on "servanthood." He wove his remarks into the unifying and organizing role of CCOP. "Aching for the universal healing of Jesus Christ and the example of it that we saw in the non-violence of Martin Luther King . . . we too have a dream. Our dream of a new Camden is a vision that rose up from the people. No outside experts came in to do it. It rose from the people and is affirmed by the people of Camden."

Faith-based organizing in Camden is probably best summed up in that servanthood practiced by clergy and church members. In spite of great diversity—religious, racial, political, ethnic, and economic—a deeper faith-based unity has been reached. Msgr. McDermott likened this unity in diversity to the Christian doctrine of the Trinity. God is a community of persons but so intimately united in love as to be one. Unity in diversity is the root, not only of our belief, but of the "free space" that faith-based organizing provides.

That unity in diversity was threatened over the issue of state intervention. However, CCOP's biblical base and Catholic Social Teaching provided guidance. First, local leaders and pastors led their communities through a prayerful process of examining the "signs of the times"—beginning with the facts, the reality of everyday life. What was happening to their city? Were local efforts and projects enough to turn Camden around? In a very real sense, people first had to "see" and understand the deeper, structural issues. Second, local people and congregations had to "judge" the issues, using Scripture and church teaching to help them to interpret their sufferings and hopes. Finally, difficult decisions had to be made about what to do about the situation. The harsh reality had to be faced: power would not be given, it had to be taken. The people had to exercise their own power. They had to "act."

To build up the city, the place where human communities exist, to create new modes of neighborliness and relationships, to perceive an original application of social justice and to undertake responsibility for this collective future, which is foreseen as difficult, is a task in which Christians must share. (Pope Paul VI, *A Call to Action*, 1971, no. 12.)

This process of "see-judge-act" has been carried out along Camden's Way of the Cross. It has meant servanthood and suffering but always with a joyful eye on Resurrection. Even after thirty years of Good Fridays and a city on life support, the community did not lose sight of Easter.

What does CCOP's struggle have to say to the rest of us? Most of us do not have to live in a city on a cross. But we might live near one or in a suburb of one. We all know of such places, if only through newspapers or TV. Nonetheless, just as the early church was largely an urban phenomenon, so is the U.S. Catholic Church. For the old ethnic immigrants as well as the newer African-American and Latino arrivals, ours is a city church. The sheer weight of history has called Catholic Christians to a role of responsibility in our urban centers. Camden's churches have responded heroically. But why should the rest of us go to bat for run-down inner city neighborhoods? Part of the answer to that question is revealed in Camden's plight and CCOP's response to that plight.

In a very real sense, the Camdens of our country have been made scapegoats that have suffered the collateral damage from surrounding communities. As an urban planner working in Camden pointed out to me, "The city has absorbed the prisoners, the garbage, the raw sewage, and the unwanted polluting industries for the whole area and really receives little or no remuneration. The surrounding area could never reimburse the city for the services it provides."

We need to ask the question, have we made scapegoats of our urban centers? We all gain from cities which do our dirty work and heavy lifting, but too often our gains condemn children to poverty, pollution, and crime. CCOP helps us to focus on a major issue—the need to evaluate support for cities in a wider regional and national context.

We all know how Jesus wept over Jerusalem in fear for the destruction of the city and its children. We too should weep for and with the Camdens of our country. But we need to do more than weep. We need to look for ways to respond.

Like Camden's Christians, we too are all called to be servants and share in solidarity the responsibility for our urban centers. The reflection on servanthood addressed to the city's residents concluded with a plea we all need to hear: "You are the servants of God in a city that is the casualty of the so-called progress of North America. Sometimes, the city feels like Ground Zero in the uphill struggle of human hope and urban development. It is very likely the worst city in America. 'A city in darkness waiting . . . in labor for the birth of a new day.'" Let us pray that Camden's new day has begun.

Every Sunday, Catholic Christians gather together to reenact the life, death, and resurrection of Jesus and share His body. That shared body, the Eucharist, commits us to the poor, to servanthood, and to the "birth of a new day." If we take that sacramental vision seriously, then we should work in solidarity with efforts like CCOP to get our suffering inner cities off the cross.

DISCUSSION QUESTIONS

1. Discuss what you think about services in your community: police, schools, health, recreation, social services. How do they compare to Camden?
2. Who/what do you think is responsible for Camden's plight? How should neighboring counties or suburbs respond?
3. How do you think faith-based community organizing, like that of CCOP, might relate to prayer, Mass, and sacraments?
4. Discuss the Catholic social principles of solidarity, subsidiarity, and participation in light of Camden. Can you think of examples in your area where these principles might apply? How? Why?
5. CCOP uses the term "action" when speaking of large community meetings. Is this "action" approach Christian? Are you comfortable with the "struggle" implied in community action?
6. How do you define power? Who has power in your community, parish, city? Discuss CCOP's principle "power is taken not given." How does that compare to your experience?
7. Is there an American urban policy? Does your state have an urban policy? Should there be such policies? What do you think should go into such policies? How might one go about educating oneself or one's parish about urban problems?

SUGGESTED PARISH ACTION

Contact the Romero Center, a social justice education center located in Camden, New Jersey. Arrange for a CCHD Journey to Justice retreat or another justice education program. The Romero Center is a ministry of St. Joseph Pro-Cathedral. The center can provide an immersion experience in the kind of work which the CCOP is doing and of "faith-based organizing." For parishes too far from Camden, your diocesan CCHD director can advise you of other urban retreat centers and help arrange a CCHD "journey to justice."

CONTACTS

Camden Churches Organized for People
2770 Federal Street
Camden, NJ 08105
856-966-8869

The Romero Center
2907 Federal Street
Camden, NJ 08105
romerocenter@comcast.net
www.rc.net/camden/stjoseph

For information on the "Journey to Justice" process or to contact your CCHD diocesan director, use the CCHD's website: *www.usccb.org/cchd*

OPTIONAL FURTHER STUDY

Annie E. Casey Foundation, *A Path Forward for Camden: Situation Analysis* (Baltimore: Annie E. Casey, June 2001).

Catholic Campaign for Human Development, *Way of the Cross: Toward Justice and Peace,* Faith and Human Development Series (Washington, DC: USCC, 1997).

Philip J. Chmielewski, S.J., "Community Organization" in Judith A. Dwyer, ed., *The New Dictionary of Catholic Social Thought* (Collegeville, MN: Liturgical Press, 1994), pp. 210–214.

Sean Closkey and Pilar Hogan, "Building Houses, Educating Communities: A Praxis/Reflection Model," *Living Light* (Summer 1999), pp. 38–43.

Dennis A. Jacobsen, *Doing Justice: Congregations and Community Organizing* (Minneapolis: Fortress Press, 2001).

Thomas Massaro, S.J., *Living Justice: Catholic Social Teaching in Action* (Franklin, WI: Sheed and Ward, 2000), pp. 119–132; pp. 209–214.

Gregory F. Augustine Pierce, *Activism That Makes Sense: Congregations and Community Organization* (Chicago: ACTA Publications, 1984).

Meredith Ramsey, "Redeeming the City: Exploring the Relationship between Church and Metropolis," *Urban Affairs Review* 33 (May 1998), pp. 595–626.

Mark Warren, *Dry Bones Rattling: Community Building to Revitalize Democracy* (Princeton: Princeton University Press, 2001).

Richard Wood, *Faith in Action: Religion, Race, and Democratic Organizing in America* (Chicago: University of Chicago Press, 2002).

4

✛

Stop the Factory Farms: Southeast Iowa Citizens for Community Improvement

Davis County, Iowa

SETTING: THE POLLUTION OF A WAY OF LIFE

As the Humane Society reminds us, hog farming in the U.S. has produced some charming characters. "Wilbur" in the children's classic *Charlotte's Web* and the more recent "Babe" of Golden Globe fame have captured the imagination of the American public—both young and old. But on a recent visit to Davis County in Southeast Iowa, I was exposed to a very different symbol of the hog industry. A huge semitrailer rolled down the single-lane gravel road. It was one of the giant trailer trucks of a large pork company on its way to the slaughterhouse in nearby Ottumwa. Normally, the smaller vehicles on the road, usually farmers' pick-up trucks, are compelled to pull into the ditch, bite the dust, and let the big truck pass. This time, however, Frank and Jodi Jones, a farm couple and founding members of the Southeast Chapter of Iowa Citizens for Community Improvement (CCI) decided to hold their ground. Perhaps because Frank was armed with a video camera, a peculiar thing happened. The semi abruptly stopped and slowly backed up. This occurrence is not especially significant until it is placed in the wider context of what is happening to the family farm and to rural Iowa. "Wilbur" and "Babe"— and smaller, environmentally sound farms—are being run over by corporate tractor trailers!

Although hog production nationwide increased by 28 percent between 1992 and 1997, the number of hog farms dropped by 46 percent. This trend—toward high-density corporate farms—is evident in Iowa and especially in Davis County. Family farms are closing, air and water are being polluted, fish are being killed, and young people no longer want to farm or can't afford to. Iowa farmers have paid dearly to make their state the nation's leading pork producer. The change from independent farmers raising a few hundred hogs in outdoor pens in an open field to corporations raising thousands in large, closed confinement buildings has turned neighbor against neighbor and caused major community, economic, and environmental problems. According to Brother David Andrews, C.S.C., of National Catholic Rural Life Conference, our food system is being consolidated into the hands of a few large companies. He referred to the business concept of "vertical integration." "Instead of a system of distinct economic units intersecting—the farmer, the wholesaler, the processor, and the retailer—you have only one huge system where everything is owned by just a few companies." What this means for the small farmer is that it is not just the air and water that are being polluted, it is a whole way of life.

I learned of this averted road rage while on a Catholic Campaign for Human Development "Journey to Justice" retreat with sixteen students from the University of Iowa's Newman Center.

> The development of solidarity through education is . . . a goal of the CCHD's Journey to Justice process. As part of this process, middle- and upper-income parishioners participate in a retreat designed to break down barriers that separate groups of people along income lines. The retreat format—the first phase of the process—includes an "immersion" experience with people from a CCHD-funded project. In the second phase of the process, the two groups are brought together to build relationships around mutual interests and concerns. (CCHD, *Principles, Prophecy, and a Pastoral Response*, 2001, 28.)

The students visited Davis County to gain firsthand experience of the contentious issue of the large "factory farms" and the organizing work going on in defense of the small farmer. The plight of the family farmer was viewed under the light of Catholic Social Teaching, especially the Church's preferential option for and with the poor, structural sin, solidarity, and care for the environment.

Frank and Jodi found the strength to hold their ground because of their involvement with Iowa Citizens for Community Improvement (CCI). The statewide organization was founded in 1976 with the purpose of uniting people, especially lower-income people, living in cities, small towns, and rural areas to support positive social, economic, and environmental change in their communities. It offers training and technical assistance to local groups to take on some of the toughest issues in rural areas including farm credit, sustainable agriculture, and, most importantly, the problems which result from the large, corporate-owned Confined Animal Feeding Operations (CAFOs) often referred to as "Factory Farms."

The Catholic Campaign for Human Development has supported the effort to establish a Southeast Chapter of Iowa Citizens for Community Improvement covering Davis, Wapello, Van Buren, and Appanoose counties. As Garry Klicker, a farmer and owner of a local grocery store in Bloomfield, the seat of Davis County, pointed out, the local concerned citizens' group was powerless when confronted by the large out-of-state corporations "who came into the county, bought up farms, and installed monstrous, polluting farm factories." Often it was difficult even to find out who the investors were.

> Woe to those who enact unjust statutes
> and who write oppressive decrees,
> Depriving the needy of judgment
> and robbing my people's poor of their rights (Is 10:1–2).

The Davis County group needed training, support, and technical assistance, and so they affiliated with the statewide organization.

During a meeting with the chapter's leaders, it was clear that this was a group of people who have known one another for years. They relate to one another and across generations as family. Blanche, seventy-five years old, candidly described the pressure one of the large pork companies put on her to sell her farm land. "They seemed even to know how much I owed at the bank," she said. As a widow, she was vulnerable to the hardsell, but she held her ground. She told the company representative, "Do what you want . . . I'm not selling." What troubles Blanche most was the social and psychological impact that the large corporate farms were having on the local community. When her husband died, her neighbors helped her "get out the crop" and got her through the crisis.

> Bear one another's burdens, and so you will fulfill the law of Christ (Gal 6:2).

She fears that "money and production efficiency" are melting the solidarity that bonded their community together. Ernie and Dee, longtime Davis County farmers, explained that young farmers were being "hoodwinked" into thinking they would get rich quick by contracting with large hog producers. "They end up not as farmers, but as low-level hired hands with large debts and low income."

Peggy spoke about the horrible smell coming off the large hog confinements, especially during periods when manure is being spread. For at least two weeks a year, she cannot even go outside. She and her husband move to the basement. She packs her two teenage children off to their grandparents. The stench from the five hog sites around her farm as well as the "dead pig" storage facility is overpowering her and her family. Frank chimed in that the smell would "gag a maggot." Jodi sadly spoke of her neighbor, "he suffers from emphysema and is on oxygen. . . . Everytime one of the facilities spreads manure, he is driven from his home. The horrible stench and toxic fumes coming from the facilities make him sicker than he already is. He can't breathe even with the oxygen."

Jodi raised the troubling issue of methamphetamine addiction which has affected a number of young people, especially women. She discussed CCI's support of a group called "Moms Off Meth" which is rallying local residents, area businesses, and law enforcement agencies to address drug problems. Anhydrous ammonia, a fertilizer which is also used to manufacture methamphetamines, is stolen from farms and easily cooked into a potent drug. Many families have been overcome with financial worries, unemployment, and despair. Increased drug use has been one outcome of this stress-filled situation. Community and family are eroding just like the air, water, and soil. That is why the red stop signs reading "Stop the Factory Farms" pepper the farm lands more and more.

Here was an unlikely group of activists who raise funds through cake sales and church potluck suppers putting themselves on the line to protect a way of life. Their love of the land and responsibility for its care echoed Leviticus, "The land shall not be sold in perpetuity; for the land is mine, and you are but aliens who have become my tenants. Therefore, in every part of the country that you occupy, you must permit the land to be redeemed" (Lv 25:23–24). Their interest in participation, more local control, and concern for family and the environment fits well with Catholic Social Teaching. While few voices have been raised in defense of the small farmer, the group is grateful for the strong stance of many Midwestern Catholic Bishops.

Bloomfield, with its picturesque county courthouse and cozy town square surrounded by rolling hills and cornfields, does not conjure up images of poverty or "a culture of death." After all, Iowa is the "field of dreams" state. Why has it been so targeted by big agribusiness? Why Davis County? These were the questions that were raised by the university students. They were surprised to meet poor people who looked just like their parents and grandparents. So was I!

[W]e urge citizens, local, state and federal government and all persons of good will to: seriously examine and, if necessary, restrict the operation of large scale animal confinement operations, looking not only at ownership and environmental questions, but also how such operations affect the common good of the community;

Some may dismiss such actions and concerns as contrary to the notions of "progress" and "efficiency." To them, the loss of family farms and vertical integration is inevitable. The economy, however, is a human-made institution and not an inevitable force. Moreover, in his encyclical, *The Gospel of Life*, Pope John Paul II reminds us that when cultural, economic and political currents encourage an idea of society excessively concerned with efficiency, a conspiracy against life is unleashed and a "culture of death" is promoted. We cannot embrace such a culture in the name of progress. (Roman Catholic Bishops of North Dakota on the crisis in rural life, *Given Thanks through Action*, 2000.)

Davis County is indeed vulnerable. The population is only 8,300 people, and it is one of the poorest counties in the state. The number of hog farmers has been decreasing every year—from 254 in 1987 to 94 in 1997. There are about 70 now. And yet, like the national trend, actual hog production remains constant. Fewer and fewer farmers are producing the same number of hogs. In the last few years, hog prices paid to farmers have plummeted to historic lows. The net income of Iowa's farmers has been cut in half. According to United States Department of Agriculture (USDA) statistics, over one-third of the households in rural midwestern counties have an annual income of less than $15,000 per year. More and more, survival for the independent farmer means both husband and wife take off-farm jobs, when they can be found. They work the farm in the early morning, evenings, and weekends. No time is left for family and community concerns.

The farm economy can never be developed solely according to the principles of maximum production and highest profit. Rather the respectful care of the land, plants and animals in accord with God's plan, which is best carried out by farmers working together in local communities, must guide agricultural economic development. (*U.S. Catholic*, March 2002, Bishop Raymond L. Burke of LaCrosse, Wisconsin, President of the National Catholic Rural Life Conference.)

In Iowa, and across the county, farm communities are facing a social, economic, and environmental crisis. As Bob Zyskowski points out in *U.S. Catholic*, "With the loss of family farms and a middle class comes poverty. Of the 250 poorest counties in the nation, 243 are rural counties." Davis County is indeed a microcosm of a much wider issue that affects us all.

THE FACTORY FARM AND BROKEN PROMISES

According to CCI members, in the mid nineties, Heartland Pork, one of Iowa's largest producers, came into Davis County and offered a "good neighbor" policy. Company representatives claimed they would help the local economy. The company promised benefits in exchange for the establishment of some large hog confinements. The benefits included high wages for young people who could not afford their own land and an increase in the price of corn since the hogs raised would consume large quantities of local feed. The company also held out the carrot that the earnings from the hog factories would substantially improve the county's tax base. Given these promises and in spite of some opposition, county political leaders saw economic opportunity and opened the barn door. Heartland began operations in Davis County in 1996. By 1999, nineteen new hog factories were built, modeled on hog confinements earlier established in North Carolina. Each facility confines 2,000 to 5,000 hogs.

When John Paul II visited Iowa in 1979, he encouraged us to "keep the land well." The shift toward large confinement operations in the Iowa countryside has raised serious concern for the quality of the land, water and air in our state. (Iowa Catholic Conference, *A Call to Reflect on God's Creation in Preparation for the Millennium,* 1998.)

The factory farm was a completely new and countercultural phenomenon for Davis County. The confinements are capital-intensive and require large buildings and extensive mechanical equipment. They consist of completely enclosed buildings sometimes as large as football fields where thousand of pigs are automatically herded through a process "from farrow to finish." Usually moved through two or three building sites over a four-month period in assembly-line order, pigs are born, medicated, impregnated, fed, watered, and fattened for slaughter. The floor is either concrete or made of metal slats for ready waste removal. Processing is all done mechanically and involves the minimum of "husbandry" or contact with the farmer. Hog farming has followed poultry farming into the factory model.

The obvious catch in this factory approach is the animal waste. Because of the concentrated volume, what agriculturalists call "manure management" becomes extremely important for air and water pollution as well as animal and human health. In Iowa alone, hog factories produce billions of gallons of waste every year. Pig manure in proper amounts is an effective fertilizer for many crops, but large hog factories are required to use all the manure they produce on their own fields. To avoid dangerous over-application of nitrogen and phosphorus found in the manure, factory farms must first store pig waste in large pits or lagoons on their land so the manure can decompose. These open cesspools not only give off a strong stench, they also cause air pollution. In addition, lagoons containing liquid manure are subject to cracking and seepage which have caused contamination of groundwater, wells, streams, and rivers. "In the past two years alone, over 140 manure spills and 'incidences' have been reported in Illinois, Iowa, Minnesota and Missouri. Millions of fish and other forms of aquatic life have been killed."

For the Davis County group, Heartland's promises and opportunities, like the air they breathe and the water they drink, have turned sour. They summarized their position in a report "Heartland Pork in Davis County," December 12, 2001. As for the local economy, rather than raising the local grain prices, the company's practice of bringing in its own grain from far away has caused prices to go down every year. Local property values have also plummeted. Because of the smell and air and water pollution, people simply do not want to buy a house that has a hog factory nearby. Moreover, the small family farmer now finds it harder and harder to get credit at the local bank. The so-called efficiency of the large producers is becoming the slogan used against the little guy. Studies from various state universities have documented that hog factories depress the sale value of land and homes in their vicinity and actually tend to hinder economic growth in rural communities. National Catholic Rural Life Conference (NCRLC) states: "We challenge the notion that CAFOs, particularly hog factories, are a boon to local economies. Studies have shown that for every job created by a hog factory, three are lost. Every year, hog factories put almost 31,000 farmers out of business, out of their homes and out of their communities."

The Southeast CCI report further maintained that environmentally Heartland Pork has not been a good steward. Toxic fumes from their facilities are making people sick. The corporation promised it would "knife" in all of the manure, which means plowing it into the soil. This has not happened and Iowa's Department of Natural Resources has received numerous complaints of irresponsible applications.

In 1997, a University of Iowa study found that residents who lived near large hog factories reported significantly more respiratory problems. In 2002, this was confirmed in a joint study by University of Iowa and Iowa State University that "hydrogen sulfide and ammonia from factory farms are making neighbors sick." Based on these environmental studies, CCI is challenging Iowa's Department of Natural Resource to take up immediately the issue of air quality standards.

> The whole human race suffers as a result of environmental blight, and generations yet unborn will bear the cost for our failure to act today. But . . . it is the poor and the powerless who most directly bear the burden of current environmental carelessness. (U.S. Catholic Bishops, *Renewing the Earth,* 1992, 2.)

An additional issue for CCI members is the irresponsible overuse by corporate producers of antibiotics in the raising and fattening of hogs. "A recent Union of Concerned Scientists study estimates that seventy percent of antibiotics in the U.S. are used in healthy pigs, poultry, and beef cattle." The danger is that overuse of antibiotics in livestock will contribute to the development of resistance to antibiotics in humans.

The farmers of Southeast Iowa are not naïve. They realize there is no simple solution to the nationwide agricultural and livestock problems. Stemming the rural exodus demands careful economic, environmental, and social initiatives. Nonetheless, CCI feels strongly that the deck is loaded in favor of big agribusiness. Factory farming has benefited from governmental and legislative decisions. A mandatory "check-off"—a private tax deducted from the price of every pig sold in the U.S., which was originally intended to support the pork industry and farmers—now is used almost entirely to finance projects of the large agribusiness pork producers. Likewise, local and state laws in Iowa, intended to protect the individual farmer and the environment, have been amended to protect and exempt factory farms. For example, Iowa CCI continues to oppose a state law that grants a tax break, ostensibly for pollution control, to factory farms that have manure pits and lagoons. For the small farmer, Iowa's field of dreams is not level.

Much of CCI's work, especially concerning the farm factories, relates to the state legislature. The organization has presented four very modest demands by which they hope to level the playing field:

1. A moratorium on construction of new factories or expansion of existing factory farms until more is known about their impact

2. Improved air quality requiring the same clean air standards as those of the state of Minnesota
3. Stricter enforcement of air and water quality control and an increase in fines for pollution violation
4. Return to some local control so that county leaders can keep out or at least restrict factory farms.

These four modest concerns echo the views of Frank, Blanche, and Gary, and all of the CCI members. They want to participate in the decisions that affect their lives. Ironically, they represent the "rugged individualist" strain in American life. They are the kind of people who often pit themselves against "big government." They see government as the "agent of last resort." Nonetheless, their views reflect a long-standing principle of Catholic Social Teaching—subsidiarity and the proper role of government. The eventual goal and probably best solution to the placement and control of CAFOs is some form of local control but at present a higher authority needs to protect the local community and contain the environmental damage. When local people cannot perform a necessary function, the next higher levels—state or national government—need to step in to assure the common good. Environmental health concerns are a prime example where this principle needs to be applied. Pope John Paul II tells us: "It is the task of the state to provide for the defense and preservation of the common goods such as the natural and human environments, which cannot be safeguarded simply by market forces" (*The Hundredth Year*, 1991, #40).

Cardinal George of Chicago recently applied the Pope's concerns to the farm situation in the U.S. by calling for a moratorium on CAFOs in Illinois. "At some point in time, we crossed the line and some of these facilities became factories, not farms as we know them. We believe now is the time for the General Assembly to pass legislation that will halt construction of any new large-scale facilities . . . until solutions can be developed that will address the impact these facilities are having on the environment and on small farmers."

In Davis County, Southeast Iowa CCI is the only voice for the small and intermediate-sized farm. Their down-home style of organizing local folks is slowly but surely gaining resonance in the area. With the help of the Catholic Campaign for Human Development and the Diocese of Davenport, the organization has mobilized a cross section of farm families, churches, and environmental groups. Their message is clear: Farming is more than a business; it is stewardship. That stewardship affects everyone who breathes, eats, and drinks. Farm issues should be of concern to all Americans, rural and urban. Our health depends on it.

ACTIVITIES AND ACCOMPLISHMENTS

The Southeast Chapter of Iowa Citizens for Community Improvement is a new chapter, only formally begun in 1999. In this short time they have worked hard for family values, community, and the environment. Their accomplishments include:

- Led campaign to hold factory farms accountable for damage to county roads from trailer trucks
- Worked on Iowa-wide "Support Family Farms" campaign
- Led information submission to Iowa's Department of Natural Resources concerning Heartland Pork manure application violations. The department issued a notice of violation to the company and demanded revision of manure management plans
- Led a phone and letter-writing campaign to state legislators to defeat a bill which would have prevented the establishment of air quality rules for factory farms. Bill was defeated in June 2001
- Assisted statewide CCI with the collection of over 6,000 signatures for a petition to reduce air pollution—2001

EVALUATION/IMPACT

The Southeast Chapter of Iowa Citizens for Community Improvement is part of a state-wide effort. The new chapter has already made impact well beyond its immediate members. The chapter has emphasized recruiting and training leaders who can help the poor stand up for themselves in the face of family, community, economic, and environmental issues that have emerged in the wake of the proliferation of corporate-owned hog factories. There are 65,108 people in the four-county area who can benefit from the chapter's efforts because the whole area has been hit by diminished income, farm closings, drug use, and air and water pollution.

Moreover, the issue of the hog factories and the call for a moratorium on new sites has become a nationwide campaign—of importance to every American. Professor John Ikerd of the University of Missouri likened the concerns over large animal confinements and the need for agricultural and environmental sustainability to the Civil Rights movement. "The first rural community to declare and defend the fundamental moral and ethical right of its people to determine how land is used may be remembered much as Rosa Parks is remembered for refusing to move to the back of the bus in Montgomery."

REFLECTION

It was a moving experience to reflect on the work of the Southeast Iowa CCI from the perspective of sixteen university students. The collegians took the "Journey to Justice" very seriously. The Catholic Campaign for Human Development facilitators guided them through a process referred to as the "Pastoral Circle." The participants began by "inserting" themselves into the lived experience of Davis County—what the people were feeling, how they were responding. In short, they saw, they listened, they smelled. From there they moved on to a kind of "social analysis." What about the political, economic, and social factors? Who holds the power? How are decisions made? Do they have a voice? From that understanding they were led to a theological reflection on what they observed. What light do the Gospels, Catholic Social Teaching, and the movement of the Holy Spirit in a community shed on this situation? What do you think Jesus would say about this situation? Finally the group moved to the purpose of the circle—the bottom line. How should *we* respond to this situation? What action, based on *our* reflection, should *we* take—not only in the short term, but also in the long term?

We ask the Catholic community: How are we called to care for God's creation? How may we apply our social teaching, with its emphasis on the life and dignity of the human person, to the challenge of protecting the earth, our common home? What can we in the Catholic community offer to the environmental movement, and what can we learn from it? How can we encourage a serious dialogue in the Catholic community—in our parishes, schools, colleges, universities, and other settings—on the significant ethical dimensions of the environmental crisis? (U.S. Catholic Bishops, *Renewing the Earth*, 1991, p. 3.)

For some of the students it was a bumpy journey that led back home. It was a journey that also led the group into a deeper and different understanding of the Church's "preferential option for the poor," the notion of "social or structural sin," and Catholic concern for God's creation.

Many young eyes, and a few older ones, were opened by the "immersion" weekend with the people of Davis County. Students began with a somewhat stereotypical view of the poor as haggard and homeless. They were invited by the first presenter to shift their perspective to the situation of southeast Iowa with its Amish community, its Latino immigrants working in the meatpacking plants, and, most directly, family farmers slowly but surely being squeezed off their land. It was an eye-opening experience for the college students because the farm families didn't look poor, but poor they were. The farm income in the area is well below Iowa's average. As noted above, many farm families in the area scrape by on less than $15,000 per year.

But material poverty is only part of the story. For Blanche and Dee, the nagging pain of poverty comes from the lack of choice, the lack of partic- ipation they experience in the decisions that affect their lives, their fami- lies, and their community. Before they organized themselves, they were powerless. That was the most agonizing poverty. On reflection, the stu- dents realized that the people they met might be poor by wealth and in- come standards, but they were rich in human dignity and dedication to family, community, environment, and social justice. And they were will- ing to stand up and be counted for their values. The students were ex- posed to the empowered poor and to the mission of the Catholic Cam- paign for Human Development.

It was a beautiful, grace-filled experience to see how this "power"— forthright but gentle—functions in the community. It was rural America's retelling of St. Paul's Body of Christ: "If one part suffers, all parts suffer with it; if one part is honored, all the parts share its joy" (1 Cor 12:26).

After seeing and indeed smelling the plight of Davis County farmers, many of the students reflected on their own family lives. The candor of the young was contagious. The situation was much closer to home than anyone might have guessed. Frank and Jodi or Gary and Peggy could be their parents. One participant said Blanche reminded her of the "perfect, feisty grandma." A student reflected that she now understood her own family better. She said she remembered her mother recently telling her that her "shares in the family farm are worth nothing." A short time later her father was compelled to sell his land and take an off-farm job. Large hog factories had moved into her Iowa county. She recounted how sad it was because "all her dad ever wanted to be was a hog farmer." She had been oblivious to her own family's fragile economic situation and now understood better what was happening at home and across Iowa. An- other student wondered out loud if the high incidence of asthma and bronchial problems in her family and community could be related to the large hog confinements that now peppered her Iowa county. Virtually all of the students chimed in with personal reflections of no longer being able to see the poor as strange or foreign.

Poverty had indeed come very close to home. So had the Church's pref- erential option for the poor. The diocesan director of CCHD pointed out that the "option" was not an exclusive option that alienates and accuses the non-poor but rather expresses the kind of concern a family shows for a sick or injured child. The U.S. Bishops' pastoral *Economic Justice for All* resonated across the barnyards of Davis County:

The "option for the poor," therefore, is not an adversarial slogan that pits one group or class against another. Rather it states that the deprivation and powerlessness of the poor wounds the whole community. The extent of their sufferings is a measure of how far we are from being a true community of persons. These wounds will be healed only by greater solidarity with the poor and among the poor themselves. (U.S. Catholic Bishops, *Economic Justice for All*, 1986, no. 88.)

Indeed, communities in southeast Iowa have been wounded. A CCHD facilitator led the students through a theological reflection on what they had seen and heard. The concept of social and structural sin casts a wide shadow. The small farmer is caught in a web of economic, political, and environmental issues that can only be described as "sinful." The web of policies and laws—some of which started out with good intentions have become structural traps. One of the farm wives referred to the "many little things" that left us all "stuck in molasses." Her homey reference led right into Pope John Paul's treatment of the "structures of sin." Structural or social sin is rooted in personal sin and concrete acts but gets solidified in laws, regulations, taxes, and business and government practices that flow from an "all-consuming desire for profit and . . . the thirst for power" (*Sollicitudo Rei Socialis*, 1988, #36–37).

For the Holy Father, the "structure of sin" is a question of "moral evil," the fruit of "many sins." The "molasses" reference was perfect! The students were able to apply this to the environmental degradation that is happening as a result of the large hog factories. The concern for clean air, soil, and water and the importance of a healthy environment for future generations united the community's concerns with the students and dovetailed perfectly with Catholic Social Teaching on care for God's creation. In *Renewing the Earth*, our Bishops call upon Catholics to see the environmental crisis as a moral challenge. In a sense we are all faced with the same crisis as the farmers of Davis County. We all need to examine how we share the earth's resources and what we pass on to our children and grandchildren.

The students seemed to grasp the need to take up responsibility as God's stewards and co-creators. They were also very honest in their assessment of their own complicity in "structural sin" and candid in admitting their participation in certain kinds of exploitation. One student said she began the weekend thinking that the "option for the poor" was a box to be checked on a tax form! She was changed by wrestling more deeply with the story of the Good Samaritan in the context of the people of Southeast Iowa. The road to Bloomfield, just like the one to Jericho, was filled with unexpected surprises—who turned out to be neighbors.

The farm families of Davis County who oppose the large hog confinements are fighting to save a way of life. But their fight is not a nostalgic return to the "good old days" or an attempt to simply blame big business. Rather they are seeking some balance among business, government, and small independent farmers. In a very real sense they are fighting for all Americans in that the small and medium size farm constitutes our best chance to protect our water, food, and environment. The issue is much larger than Davis County. The organization's call for a moratorium on new large confinement sites, concern for the environment, and return to some local control reflect the Catholic principles of participation, subsidiarity, and care for creation. The National Catholic Rural Life Conference in 1997, and numerous Bishops since, has also called for a moratorium and a national dialogue on sustainable and environmentally responsible agriculture and livestock policy.

> We are convinced that current trends in the food sector are not in the best interests of the United States or of the global community. The decline in the number of moderate-sized farms, increased concentration of land ownership, and the mounting evidence of poor resource conservation raise serious questions of morality and public policy. As pastors, we cannot remain silent while thousands of farm families caught in the present crisis lose their homes, their land, and their way of life. (U.S. Bishops, *Economic Justice for All*, 1986, no. 231.)

Each of us, especially city and suburban residents, need to become more aware of the plight of the small and middle-size farmer. When the farm bill comes before Congress, every American should be concerned, not just farmers. For example, the farm bill passed in May 2002, will significantly increase subsidies to large commodity producers but will do little or nothing for the small farmer of Davis County. The National Catholic Rural Life Conference readily acknowledges the bill's positive aspects dealing with conservation, nutrition, and immigrant farm workers, but fears that "today's political tradeoff will lead to pain and sadness in the countryside. . . . The NCRLC laments the lack of vision in U.S. agricultural policy, but the passage of the 2002 farm bill does not end the struggle for social justice."

It is in our best interest that government invest in and support smaller and environmentally sound farms. And as Brother David Andrews reminds us, "the fork is a powerful lever." We need to be more sensitive and careful about our food choices, become "conscientious eaters," and pay attention to food labeling and agriculture and food policy. We might have to patronize the local farmers' market. We might even have to pay a little more for bacon. In the final analysis maybe a few cents a pound is the only defense against the manure pits!

We are faced with two very different systems of hog production. One model is based on "vertical integration" and maximization of profit; the other is modeled on the smaller- and intermediate-sized farm and requires a great deal more animal care and marketing skills. The latter as we have seen most clearly relates to the values of family, neighbor, environment, and social justice.

All of us need to understand the long-term implications of the current trends. The real question should not be, "How do we save family farms?" Rather we should be asking, "Which system of agriculture would best ensure safe and accessible food, would respect and protect creation, would support rural communities, and would ensure justice for producers and laborers?" These are the ingredients of an agricultural and environmental ethic that Dr. Bernard Evans draws from Catholic Social Teaching. They should be the ingredients that go into our public policy and buying habits.

Like "Wilbur" and "Babe," environmental concerns seem to have ignited a spark in the imaginations of the young, and rightly so, but what about the rest of us? How do we forge the vital holistic connections among environment, economy, and faith? Between our creator and creation? Our whole food system is dependent on a way of life now in jeopardy. But David Andrews and NCRLC are right: the fork is indeed a powerful lever. "Change could happen if people . . . would think about how the food got to their fork, about whom they bought it from, and about what impact this food has on the environment, on farmers, on their own nutrition. Eating is a moral act."

DISCUSSION QUESTIONS

1. How do you define poverty? How did the folks in Davis County show you another side to being poor?
2. Discuss the different approaches to hog production raised in this case study. What values do you think are represented by the different approaches?
3. What do you think "structural sin" is? Give some examples from your own experience. Discuss the story of the Good Samaritan in the context of structural sin.
4. Why do you think Catholic Social Teaching puts emphasis on local control and participation?
5. Discuss how Catholic social principles might be of help when economic opportunity and environmental concerns conflict.
6. What are some reasons we should all be concerned about a federal farm bill? How might government support smaller, environmentally sound farms?

7. Discuss some of your buying habits. Do you pay attention to labels and to the origin of the food products that are sold at your supermarket? Would you be willing to learn more about the pork chops you eat? Would you be willing to pay more for products raised in a healthier environmental context?

SUGGESTED PARISH ACTION

As a parish community look for opportunities to support local farmers' markets. Find out where your congressional representative stands on farm legislation and support for smaller, environmentally sound farms. Contact the National Catholic Rural Life Conference for a copy of their *Catholics on Factory Farms: Moratorium on Animal Confinement Facilities* to see how you might join the nationwide effort to stop the proliferation of large hog confinements.

CONTACTS

National Catholic Rural Life Conference
4625 Beaver Avenue
Des Moines, Iowa 50310-2199
515-270-2634
www.ncrlc.com

Southeast Chapter of Iowa Citizens for Community Improvement
P.O. Box 105
Milton, IA 52570

Iowa Citizens for Community Improvement—State Office
2001 Forest Avenue
Des Moines, IA 50311
www.IowaCCI.org

For information on the "Journey to Justice" process or to contact your CCHD diocesan director, use the CCHD website: *www.usccb.org/cchd*

OPTIONAL FURTHER STUDY

Melanie Adcock, D.V.M., and Mary Finelli, "Against Nature: The Sensitive Pig versus the Hostile Environment of the Modern Pig Farm," a reprint from *HSUS News*, Spring 1996 (The Humane Society of the United States).

Drew Christiansen, S.J., and Walter Granger, *"And God Saw That It Was Good": Catholic Theology and the Environment* (Washington, DC: USCC, 1996).

Janel M. Curry, Ph.D., "Industrial Hog Farms vs. God's Desire for Shalom," *Creation Care: A Christian Environmental Quarterly* 15 (Fall 2001), pp. 12–13.

Bernard Evans, "Agriculture and Catholic Social Teaching," *Catholic Rural Life* 43 (Spring 2001), pp. 12–17.

Thomas Massaro, S.J., *Living Justice: Catholic Social Teaching in Action* (Franklin, WI: Sheed and Ward, 2000), pp. 158–163; pp. 211–215; pp. 226–231.

Bob Zyskowski, "A Tough Row to Hoe: How Agribusiness Is Taking the Family out of Farming" and "Lift Your Fork to Help a Farmer: An Interview with Brother David Andrews, C.S.C.," *U.S. Catholic* 67 (March 2002), pp. 12–18; pp. 20–23.

5

Ladders to Success: The Anti-Displacement Project

Springfield, Massachusetts

SETTING: FROM TENANTS TO OWNERS

From the 1960s to the 1980s, landlords were awarded generous mortgage conditions from the Department of Housing and Urban Development (HUD) in exchange for keeping rents low and public-sponsored housing well-managed. By the late 1980s, as mortgage periods came to an end, low-income families were confronted with the massive loss of affordable housing. Owners opted out of the affordable housing business, either by letting buildings deteriorate and declining further federal contracts, or by simply paying off mortgages and raising rents to whatever the market would bear. In many parts of the county, poorer tenants found themselves on the street.

However, in western Massachusetts, at least in part, something very different happened.

The Anti-Displacement Project (ADP), founded in 1988 took up the role of community advocate and informed tenants of their rights in the face of potential market and condo conversions. Springfield and surrounding counties became a testing ground for a rather odd couple, pairing "subsidized housing with an unexpected mate: the by-your-bootstraps notion that poor people must take charge of their own circumstances."

Indeed, with ADP's leadership, housing became much more than a roof overhead—it came to symbolize local people's "deepest identity" and "new relations." Affordable housing was the solid ground on which ADP would build its "ladders to success." The Catholic Campaign for Human

83

> The homeless make up a group of people that is still poorer than the poor; all of us need to help them. We are convinced that a home is much more than a simple roof over one's head. The place where a person creates and lives out his or her life, also serves to found, in some way, that person's deepest identity and his or her new relations with others. (Pope John Paul II, "Letter to Cardinal Roger Etchegarary," 1987.)

Development early on understood the dramatic need for affordable housing in the area and assisted ADP with community organization grants to mobilize tenants. ADP's work spread to three counties: Hampden, Hampshire, and Franklin. Hampden County includes the cities of Springfield and Holyoke. Hampshire County is home to five colleges: Amherst, Hampshire, Mount Holyoke, Smith, and the University of Massachusetts at Amherst. Franklin County is rural with only one small city, Greenfield.

Springfield is the population center of Western Massachusetts with over 100,000 people in a metropolitan area of half a million. The city is racially mixed with large neighborhoods of African-Americans, Italians, and Irish. There is also a growing Russian-speaking immigrant community of 25,000 people. High housing prices around the "five college" area push low-income residents into Springfield and Holyoke. Greenfield and its surrounding rural areas are principally white and, like many rural New England communities, lacking employment opportunities.

In this context, ADP takes a very innovative approach linking community organization to economic development. This creative linkage promotes and sustains lasting social, educational, and economic change. ADP's mission statement clearly sets an agenda which seeks to help the poor empower themselves.

> The ADP is a multi-issue membership-based community organization. Our mission is to organize and empower low-income families in Western Massachusetts in order to build political and economic power, achieve resident control of affordable housing, promote cooperative economic development, and create lasting social and economic change.
>
> The way we accomplish this is to create new institutions controlled by low-income people and then use our combined wealth and assets to benefit our communities.

Annual dues submitted by each member organization, depending on size and ability to pay, ensure institutional stability and financial independence. Current members consist of five tenant-owned housing cooperatives, four tenant associations, one ethnic association, and the newest member, a for-profit worker-owned business. The building of independent, dues-paying institutions, working together for common goals, serves to offset the fragility often characteristic of grassroots community organizations. In its own management and operations, ADP follows Catholic Social Teaching's principle of subsidiarity: decisions and responsibilities are, whenever possible, carried out at the level of the local community and local institutions; the larger entity has a role when the common good calls for greater regulation or intervention.

> Of its very nature the true aim of all social activity should be to help individual members of the social body, but never to destroy or absorb them. This is a fundamental principle of social philosophy, unshaken and unchangeable, (and it retains its full truth today). (Pope Pius XI, *The Reconstruction of the Social Order*, 1931, #79.)

The organization's rather unique way of operating constantly pushes forward. One leader likened it to riding a bicycle—"Stop pedaling and you fall!" ADP members are multiracial, low-wage workers without job security, often single parents pushed off welfare or senior citizens living on fixed incomes. The organization also serves a growing Russian immigrant population with high language and cultural barriers. Overall, ADP represents over 10,000 families and is led by a core of 300 seasoned leaders.

Training of leaders is a key ingredient in institution building. To date about three hundred leaders have been trained in community organizing. A network of issue-based strategy teams have been set up to work on regional concerns which grow out of one-on-one meetings. The teams are led by representatives from each member organization. They plan research and activities around practical concerns such as jobs, housing, education, and utilities.

Caroline Murray, ADP's executive director, leaves much leeway for member organizations and strategy teams. Decisions come from the rank and file, and when a united effort demands it, Caroline and ADP's leaders are not afraid to use the umbrella organization to confront the power structure. She sees her role as helping low-income people "de-mythologize" the system. She is adamant, "poor people can figure out how to buy a house and how to run a business" and ADP is a catalyst to help them. Thinking big, confronting power, and local control provide the juice for this movement. The participation and empowerment of poor people in these new institutions is the key. Members are organized, efficient, and in it for the long haul.

Mary Lou, a senior citizen and long-time resident of Greenfield Gardens, told me of the vast difference in her life that ADP has made. She moved into the housing project twenty-seven years ago, thinking she would stay for two years. She is still there and is now the vice-chair of

ADP and a very active leader of Greenfield Gardens' Home Savers Council. She spoke of her own past fears of even asking the landlord for normal repairs. When refrigerators gave out after many years, tenants wouldn't ask for replacements. Mary Lou spoke for herself, "As a single mother with a disability, I was afraid of being evicted." What a difference ADP has made. She is long over her fear and now stands up and presents the Greenfield Gardens and ADP case to HUD officials, mayors, bank presidents, and senators. Mary Lou's education came from her involvement and leadership in the long process of tenant purchase and rehabilitation of Greenfield Gardens' 202 units. But she is not resting on past victories. "It's worked for me, but it has to happen for others as well." She is now one of the principle leaders involved in ADP's evolution to a multi-issue organization.

> I will rejoice and be glad in your love,
>   once you have seen my misery,
>   observed my distress.
> You will not abandon me into enemy hands
>   but will set my feet in a free and open space (Ps 31:8–9).

Ray, a carpenter and current chair of ADP, recounted his long involvement in the tenant buyout and renovation of the 270-unit Spring Meadow project in Springfield. ADP was able to leverage $17 million through HUD assistance and tax credits. He said the project was "in shambles and literally falling down but after years of fighting the HUD bureaucracy, we got the funds for the buyout." As he led me through the housing project and proudly showed off the community recreation center and computer-equipped study room for youth, he explained how the owner-tenants' council hires and oversees a property management company. The high level of accountability was manifested in the neatly maintained common areas and the nicely painted townhouses.

> Society has a moral obligation, including governmental action where necessary, to assure opportunity, meet basic human needs, and pursue justice in economic life.
>
> Workers, owners, managers, stockholders, and consumers are moral agents in economic life. By our choices, initiative, creativity, and investment, we enhance or diminish economic opportunity, community life, and social justice. (U.S. Catholic Bishops, *Economic Justice for All: A Catholic Framework for Economic Life*, 1996, nos. 8–9.)

ADP used all kinds of creative ways to confront landowners and pressure them to sell in order to keep some housing affordable. Murray states plainly, "You need to be negotiating from a position of power. In some cases we researched owners' interests: other buildings they owned and other businesses and activities they might be involved in. Then we used direct action, going to the office with fifty people to demand a meeting, or, as we did in a few cases, taking our demands directly to him at home."

This kind of creative but controversial confrontation is perhaps best illustrated in one telling tactic. Early on in the project buyout efforts, ADP sought the help of Senator Kerry. He promised a supportive letter to the HUD secretary but failed to deliver. Writer JoAnn Dilorenzo describes what happened when Kerry came to Springfield for an AFL-CIO forum on poverty: "So the tenants showed up at the forum toting bottles of ketchup, a nod to Kerry's wife, Theresa Heinz, formerly married to a condiment heir. In the middle of Kerry's speech, they broke into a rendition of the Heinz 'Anticipation' jingle, castigating Kerry for keeping them 'wai-ai-ting' for the money. Then they walked out." The letter was promptly sent to the HUD secretary and Senator Kerry is now a strong supporter of ADP!

> The exercise of solidarity within each society is valid when its members recognize one another as persons. Those who are more influential, because they have a greater share of goods and common services, should feel responsible for the weaker and be ready to share with them all they possess. Those who are weaker, for their part, in the same spirit of solidarity, should not adopt a purely passive attitude or one that is destructive of the social fabric, but, while claiming their legitimate rights, should do what they can for the good of all. The intermediate groups, in their turn, should not selfishly insist on their particular interests but respect the interests of others. (Pope John Paul II, *On Social Concerns*, 1987, no. 39.)

This organizing approach is not afraid to take a strong stance but positions taken are carefully based on sound research and business practices. Over the years, ADP members had to master all the complexities of tenant-buyouts—a formidable task. With the "Low Income Housing Preservation and Residents Home Ownership Act" of 1990, owners could refinance mortgages, repair their buildings, and keep rents affordable, or they could sell. There was one glitch: HUD offered tenant non-profit organizations the right to purchase the properties and funding was available for buyouts. This was the hook for ADP's affordable housing campaign. After the repeal of that law, however, funding for buyouts dried up. The ADP thus turned to "tax credit" programs to assist tenants in their efforts. The tax credit is an IRS-sponsored program which allows private developers to provide initial construction or rehabilitation funding for affordable rental housing in exchange for ten years of projected tax savings. Caroline, Mary Lou, Ray, and other ADP leaders maneuvered through the miles of red tape and forged alliances with owners, developers, and local government.

They succeeded beyond anyone's expectations. Their careful mastery of federal regulations, real estate law, and business and property management has paid off. Ownership of five projects—Allen Park, Spring Meadow, Greenfield Gardens, Powdermill Village, and Whiting Farms—has been turned over to tenants through a co-op board or tenant-run nonprofit institution. Overall, more than $60 million in leveraged funds have been raised and over 2,000 at-risk units have been preserved, purchased, rehabilitated, and managed as affordable housing. In addition, ADP is negotiating for tenants to take ownership and rehabilitate Cathedral Hill, a 48-unit complex being donated by the Diocese of Springfield. ADP has secured $1.6 million in local and state funds for this cooperative effort.

Clearly, ADP has proven itself a leader in protecting housing for low-income families. It is just as clear that the organization has caused massive heartburn for landlords and politicians in Western Massachusetts. Nonetheless, ADP has gained the respect even of adversaries. The reason for this is that their method of identifying issues and confronting power is always begun with the way open to negotiation and reconciliation. They take a strong stance but, like the prophets of old, remain humble and open. "You have been told, O man, what is good, and what the Lord requires of you: Only to do the right and to love goodness, and to walk humbly with your God" (Mic 6:8). The honest humility and candor have allowed ADP to build alliances across ideological barriers that include political, business, and civic leaders. The CCHD diocesan director described how ADP has truly put into practice the core principles of Catholic Social Teaching—the option for the poor, participation, solidarity, and rights of workers. She said, "ADP functions like a family. They empower and make responsible their members, including youth and young adults who take active roles for social justice in their communities. Thank God for their work. But for ADP, there would be no affordable housing left in the area."

Should anyone press you into service for one mile, go with him for two miles. Give to the one who asks of you, and do not turn your back on him who wants to borrow (Mt 5:41–42).

In discussion with Caroline, Ray, and Mary Lou, as well as tenants, young and old, the approach and methods of ADP are hashed over and refined. The constant interaction of rights and responsibilities, confrontation and reconciliation, self-determination and community, characterizes the forward movement. Caroline readily admits: "In more traditional tenant organizing, we would've been fighting with owners over repairs. Now instead, the tenants of the building control a major asset and make day-to-day decisions about rents and repairs. They're thinking strategically, making sure all bank accounts are in local banks, for example. These tenants are more than tenants; they're major holders in the city."

> Flowing from our God-given dignity, each person has basic rights and responsibilities. . . . People have a fundamental right to life and to those things that make life truly human: food, clothing, housing, health care, education, security, social services, and employment. Corresponding to these rights are duties and responsibilities—to one another, to our families, and to the larger society, to respect the rights of others and to work for the common good. (U.S. Catholic Bishops, *A Century of Social Teaching*, 1991, p. 5.)

The emphasis on rights and responsibilities constantly pushes the organization to thorough democratic participation, self-criticism, and power sharing. Housing was clearly the fulcrum, but ADP realizes that strong and economically viable neighborhoods depend on more than housing. ADP has now moved to insure control over their own assets so that gains from the housing buyouts stay with local residents. Like most low-income neighborhoods, they experience the problem of capital flight, the process where money is sucked out of the local community. ADP expanded its horizons to economic development and the "Ladders to Success" campaign was launched.

WORKER-OWNERS: CONTROLLING ASSETS AND WORKFORCE DEVELOPMENT

The Ladders to Success campaign was launched when ADP brokered its obvious successes in community organization and housing to the broader areas of economic development, jobs, and actual wealth accumulation. The "ladder" initiative enlisted a cadre of leaders, as well as the whole membership, in the battle to keep the financial gains made in the housing buyouts flowing within the community. This means jobs, viable careers, and education. The Ladders to Success consist of a three-tiered strategy: access to job training and education; organizing low-wage workers to create a workers' center; and a long-term analysis of the regional economy in order to identify what types of business exist or could be developed to create living wage jobs and open decent career paths.

Job training and workers' rights were the first step. However, career paths and creation of new institutions controlled by poor people which keep wealth and assets in the community are the long-range goal. The apartments the residents purchased required extensive renovation. Peeling paint, broken windows, leaky plumbing, and aged appliances all needed attention. Once again, ADP's use of sweat equity came into play. Leadership saw opportunity in the mess and set out to cut a deal. For the needed renovations, the organization committed to hiring all union workers, even though it could potentially cost more. In return, local unions agreed to train, hire, and mentor ADP members in building trades positions. Some residents, like Ray, had skills but not the credentials and experience needed for construction jobs. This was certainly the case for Russian and Latino immigrants. Sixty-five ADP members were initially hired as apprentices or journeymen carpenters, electricians, painters, and laborers. Both community and unions gained from this first step. Unions increased access to new members and new job sites, and ADP members gained access to union membership and relatively high wage building trade careers.

Another component in the move to create economic opportunity was the establishment of a for-profit, worker-owned cooperative landscape business—United Landscaping Company (ULC). The ADP specifically looked for established, skilled workers such as Ray but also opened the door of opportunity to younger people. When Lee jumped out of ULC's new truck to show me the work they were doing at Spring Meadow, he beamed with the pride of a young man who had worked his way out of poverty. He could now boast not only of being a homeowner but also a business owner. His life had been turned around by the ADP vision. The landscaping and snow removal business is another successful effort at controlling and sharing community assets. The cooperatively-owned business is both a way to create jobs and a form of economic self-determination.

With a business planning grant from the CCHD, the team of potential worker-owners was recruited and during a year-long series of weekly meetings planned out the structure of the cooperative business. Working with consultants, members themselves created and wrote a business plan and marketing strategy. The business took start-up advantage of its captive market, the five member housing projects—with significant landscaping, maintenance, and snow removal needs but also leveraged strong political and economic support to secure $175,000 in start-up capital. The United Cooperative Bank of Springfield became a significant corporate sponsor and the City of Springfield willingly signed on ULC as its snow removal contractor. The thirteen worker-owners started in June 2001, with a first-year projected revenue of $500,000. By mid 2002, the workers were earning $12.00 an hour, with benefits and year-end profit-sharing.

For Lee and his children, his townhouse and ULC is the American dream come true. He told me he had just about given up on that dream, but ADP gave him and his children a new lease on life—a new hope.

During a lunch break, Lee sat across from me. His dreadlocks made him look younger than his thirty-six years. The hairdo, he explained with a proud grin, was a "creative art" project of his seven-year-old daughter. His commitment and concern for his children was apparent. Both son and daughter are active in the youth work and anti-drug and gang programs organized by ADP. Lee honestly admits that he was part of the street scene and paid too little attention to his young children and their mother. He struggled by on minimum wage jobs and constantly seeking "Temporary Assistance for Needy Families." Neither did him or his children any good. Working two minimum-wage jobs, he was not able to support his children. He applied for benefits but was denied. "You know why? They said for a family of four I earned $1.00 too much. But I was living in poverty, trying to take care of my kids and work two jobs." At the time, his yearly earnings were less than $10,000! Through ADP, Lee found a way out of poverty but more importantly he found responsibility and human dignity. "I learned that I have power and that means I have responsibility—to my children, to ADP, and to the wider community." He added that if it wasn't for ADP, "I would probably be homeless, in jail, or dead." But instead with home and job, he is a caring parent. His children are active ADP youth leaders—because, he says, they can see, "Dad's doing it."

> The family has major contributions to make in addressing questions of social justice. It is where we learn and act on our values. . . . We also have the right and responsibility to participate in and contribute to the broader communities in society. . . . (U.S. Catholic Bishops, *A Century of Social Teaching*, 1990, p. 5.)

Another important rung on the ladder focuses on the federal Workforce Investment Act (WIA). This law provides the means by which the unemployed and low-wage workers should have access to job search assistance and training through "one stop career centers." A for-profit corporation, FutureWorks, was the designated welfare one-stop job center for Springfield. However, after numerous complaints, ADP decided to "test" whether the center was fulfilling its mandate and the spirit of the WIA. ADP sent thirty-two people who identified themselves as low-wage workers, unemployed, or welfare recipients. "Testers" were representative of racial, ethnic, and national groups in the Springfield area. They made forty-two visits with specific requests such as "I want to get computer training" or "I'm looking for a job in childcare." All inquiries were clearly within the domain of the WIA mandate. After each visit, reactions and conversations were reported on and a survey sheet filled out. In what can only be considered a shocking response, *not one* of the forty-two test visits "resulted in enrollment in a skill development or training program, nor did any of them secure employment." Moreover, testers who did not speak English received no help in their native languages. The sting operation revealed a great deal about the lack of services to "families who are struggling to make ends meet."

In order to make the point about the ineffectiveness of FutureWorks, ADP presented its documented report, *FutureWorks: Roadblocks to Success* to the Regional Employment Board, and demanded a response. The evidence was so overwhelming that with the strong support of the mayor of Springfield, the "one-stop employment center" was shut down and turned over to a locally-run non-profit group controlled by an appointed board and held to stringent accountability measures. The results have been most positive: assistance for immigrants has been increased; GED classes are being offered on a regular basis; and the center's priority has turned to job training for low-income adults and youth.

Through ADP's effort, some of the profit has been taken out of welfare assistance in Western Massachusetts. People are no longer turned away or shunted from temp agency to temp agency. Some longer-range job training with career path potential has begun. While this kind of direct action organizing causes some to blanch, the willingness to stand up has made the ADP vision a reality. Access to job training is the first step and the FutureWorks victory was the first of its kind in the U.S.

It is a strict duty of justice and truth not to allow fundamental human needs to remain unsatisfied, and not to allow those burdened by such needs to perish. It is also necessary to help needy people to acquire expertise, to enter the circle of exchange, and to develop their skills in order to make the best use of their capacities and resources. (Pope John Paul II, *The Hundredth Year*, 1991, no. 34.)

Step two on the ladder concerns ADP's commitment to "contingent workers." Contingent work is a well-established feature of the American economy and refers to temporary workers, day laborers, and other low-wage workers—employed in both the private and public sector. These temporary workers are often exploited and abused because this area of employment is largely unregulated and existing laws often go unenforced. Companies and public agencies, often in a budget-cutting mode, want to avoid medical and other insurance, overtime pay, and employee benefits, and therefore move to part-time or full-time contingency workers who can easily be let go. Workers are usually hired from "temp agencies." The ADP is teaming up with AFL-CIO to examine such agencies on issues like health and safety, transportation, and wages. Rather than leave contingent workers at the mercy of temp agencies, ADP, in collaboration with the Central Labor Council of Western Massachusetts and with the support of Jobs with Justice, Western Massachusetts Legal Services, and a coalition of churches, will establish a "Workers' Center." The idea has the support of key local and state economic and political leaders of all political persuasions. The center will be a new institutional member of ADP and will provide job training and placement, a hiring hall, legal assistance, and a health care trust fund for job seekers. The center will also oversee a community fund which will offer grants to local non-profit organizations that are managing or developing programs that will enhance the workforce capacity and worker participation in business development.

While many community organizations would rest content with the housing and job opportunities ADP has created, the organization continues to push its vision. Ladders to Success evokes a broader strategy, a plan for the long-haul of economic development, including decent paying career jobs, profit-sharing by workers, control of assets, and wealth accumulation. In a very real sense, the members of ADP are imitating the normal career paths of most Americans. Just as poor people cannot be expected to rest content with slum-like housing, they cannot be expected to rest content being shipped from dead-end job to dead-end job. As our Bishops indicate, "Work is more than a way to make a living; it is an expression of our dignity and a form of continuing participation in God's creation. People have the right to decent and productive work, to decent and fair wages, to private property and economic initiative" (U.S. Catholic Bishops, *A Century of Social Teaching*, 1998, p. 7).

The third step in the Ladders to Success addresses the strategic and business planning necessitated by regional industry trends. Good business and good jobs call for sound planning and careful assessment of the regional economy. Working with a business consultant, ADP has developed a "sector employment intervention strategy." Initial research considered eight different parts of the area's economy, then honed in on three of these sectors identified by ADP's jobs strategy team as offering the best employment possibilities. The three sectors chosen were: health care, metal manufacturing, and educational support services. Each sector is being evaluated on issues such as stability and growth potential; entry-level skill requirements and training opportunities; entry-, mid-level and executive wages and benefits; turnover rates; diversity of jobs available; opportunity for advancement and career ladder; relationship of sector to organized labor; role of contingent or temporary workforce to sector; and racial and gender equity within the sector. The sectors are being assessed in collaboration with city and county government, employment and training providers, business leaders, and the chamber of commerce.

When all the data is collected and analyzed, the ADP jobs strategy team will identify one sector for intervention. The final phase of the Ladders to Success campaign will be completed in 2003. At that point, the jobs strategy team, working with the Workers' Center, city and state officials, the Workforce Investment Board, and area business and banking leaders will decide on a sector intervention and begin recruitment, training, and placement of workers.

The Catholic Campaign for Human Development has continued to support ADP because of its creative vision linking rights with responsibilities and community organization with economic development. The approach highlights Catholic Social Teachings' emphasis on participation, solidarity, worker's rights, and the option for the poor, but in a uniquely American version of social entrepreneurship combined with social justice.

> Poor and vulnerable people have a special place in Catholic social teaching. A basic moral test of a society is how its most vulnerable members are faring. (U.S. Catholic Bishops, *A Century of Social Teaching*, 1991, p. 6.)

As we have seen, ADP has not shied away from that testing of our society. Indeed, its creative and assertive approach has been attentive to a double bottom line: business and economic success *and* empowerment for the poor.

One additional programmatic activity should be noted. While not formally part of the ladder initiative, it is clearly a key ingredient to the long-range intergenerational success of ADP—education and youth leadership. At the Spring Meadow project, I met Amanda, Keith, and Sean, all teenagers who are active in the projects' youth group. They proudly showed off the project recreation center and computer lab. The young people have established a youth group with their own governing board and budget. Forty young people turn out for Friday night activities. They hold bake sales and car washes to raise money for supervised outings and activities. Lee, Keith's dad, is enthusiastic about the difference he is seeing in the teenagers. "We got wind of a new gang forming in Spring Meadow called the Canon Circle Krew, the graffiti read 'CCK.'" The youth group led by Amanda took action and walked the grounds. "It was kids talking to kids, telling them they did not want gangs, and they invited the kids to join the youth group." Three of five gang members approached joined the Spring Meadow Youth Group.

> Say not, "I am too young."
>   To whomever I send you, you shall go;
>   whatever I command you, you shall speak.
> Have no fear before them,
>   because I am with you to deliver you, says the LORD (Jer 1:7–8).

The most important accomplishment of ADP's education-youth initiative is a groundbreaking partnership they have formed with the University of Massachusetts at Amherst. When community leaders realized that for their kids, the nearby state university was a "foreign land" and that students were being "tracked away" from college courses, they decided to take action. ADP hired a full-time youth and education organizer who established a mentoring and leadership program for over one hundred young people. The program grew by leaps and bounds. Volunteers come in from surrounding colleges and tutor students at each housing project in academic and social skills. Academic achievement among the children in the projects has greatly improved. Fifty high school juniors and seniors participated in a UMass campus visit and spent the day with students and professors. Youth are paired with mentors and can sit in on classes and get a taste of college life. The campus visits are now an ongoing feature of ADP's programming. An "access to college" program has been formally established with UMass-Amherst. In September 2001, the first ADP youth was admitted to the university on scholarship. The Ladders to Success campaign is being passed on to the next generation.

The forward movement relentlessly rolls on. ADP is involved in a multi-year development plan to evaluate past accomplishments and map out new directions. It is clear that the organization has moved beyond displacement, tenant organizing, and housing issues to broader economic concerns of wealth accumulation and worker control over institutions and assets. Given the strong emphasis on economic development, the planning group is even considering a name change that would better capture the organization's current focus.

ADP's vision ignites the aspirations and imagination of its constituents as well as their business acumen. The organization seems willing to constantly challenge not only the wider power structure but also its own organizational parameters. The Ladders to Success campaign is open-ended and self-critical. ADP sees problems, not enemies, and has crossed the great divide for many community-based organizations from protest to policy. And it has done so with tactics that confront the system but with longer-range strategies that move quickly to negotiation and reconciliation. Self-interest is consistently balanced by the common good and solidarity with the poor.

ACTIVITIES AND ACCOMPLISHMENTS

ADP has proven itself a very effective advocate for low-income families mainly because of its approach to community organization and its linkage of that approach to economic development, control of assets, and wealth accumulation by low-income people.

Accomplishments include:

- Agreement reached with Regional Employment Board for 25 year-round jobs for ADP youth to work as organizers and engage in leadership training
- Cooperative control of $30 million cash flow in the local economy in 2001
- Leveraged over $60 million in federal, state, and local funds to purchase and rehabilitate over 2,000 units of affordable housing
- Implemented a labor agreement with building trades union resulting in placement of seventy-five minority poor, laborers, carpenters, and electricians
- Creation of United Landscaping Company, a for-profit business with thirteen worker-owners and first year sales of $500,000
- Established an "access to college" partnership with the University of Massachusetts at Amherst which includes mentoring, admissions, and scholarship assistance for ADP youth
- Won precedent setting agreement guaranteeing local control and accountability from the Regional Employment Board in job training and Workforce Investment Act implementation
- Designed and implemented the "Ladders to Success" campaign including job training, a workers' center, and long-term sectoral intervention strategy

EVALUATION/IMPACT

The impact of ADP has been significant for Springfield and surrounding counties. The organization has become a major economic actor in the area. It represents almost 10,000 families and is led by a core of 300 trained, experienced leaders. Most importantly, ADP has built a network of organizations led by low-income people in the crucial areas of housing, jobs, and economic development. When John Briggs, Vice President of the United Cooperative Bank of Springfield was awarding $75,000 in start-up funds for the United Landscaping Company, he neatly summed up ADP's regional impact: "They're an outstanding example of what will happen when you empower people . . ." That power is being shared throughout Western Massachusetts.

REFLECTION

The leaders of ADP—Caroline, Ray, Mary Lou, Lee, and many others—are not afraid to ask the hard questions. In defense of the poor they are not afraid to offend. Many Catholics might prefer a kinder, gentler approach. But if we reflect on our own tradition from the prophets through Jesus right down to Pope John Paul's call for worker solidarity and the right to organize, we can see that ADP has strong Catholic allies. The Pope's emphasis on the "spirituality of work" and work as sharing in God's creation mirrors ADP's ongoing Ladders to Success. People ask, "Where does ADP get its ideas, its push? How can low-income workers accomplish so much?" In a discussion of Christ, the working man, the Holy Father indicates that similar questions confronted Jesus. The Pope refers to the Gospel of Mark where Jesus' first listeners in Nazareth "were astonished, saying, 'Where did this man get all this? What is the wisdom given to him? . . . Is not this the carpenter?" (Pope John Paul II, *On Human Work*, 1991, #26).

Perhaps it would be of help for us to step back and reflect prayerfully on ADP's ladders. How do their steps relate to our own lives and lifestyles? How do we deal with housing, jobs, and personal and family responsibilities? What do we see as "wisdom" in our own everyday tough decisions? Probably, we would come to the conclusion that we admire people who stand up for themselves and ask the hard questions. We might also find out that we need to reexamine our own ambiguous stance toward power. As ADP illustrates, having power means having responsibility, and responsibility has an obligation to seek the common good. All of us are called "to speak truth to power" and we know how hard that can be. But ADP is doing just that.

The approach builds new institutions controlled by low-income people and links these institutions in a regional multi-issue organization. The ADP then has the power to compel accountability from decision makers and to act as a mediating institution for thousands of low-income families who have no other voice. John Paul II refers to such efforts:

> Positive signs in the contemporary world are the growing awareness of the solidarity of the poor among themselves, their efforts to support one another, and their public demonstrations on the social scene which, without recourse to violence, present their own needs and rights in the face of the inefficiency or corruption of the public authorities. By virtue of her own evangelical duty, the Church feels called to take her stand beside the poor, to discern the justice of their requests, and to satisfy them, without losing sight of the good of groups in the context of the common good. (Pope John Paul II, *On Social Concern*, 1988, #39.)

Although ADP is not directly linked to a church, its strong emphasis on vision has a biblical ring, ". . . where there is no vision, the people perish" (cf. Prv 29:18). Moreover, the ADP leaders are acutely aware that "without organization the vision perishes." As summed up by Dennis Jacobson, "Vision without organization is fanciful. Organization without vision is moribund." As we have seen, ADP is neither fanciful nor moribund.

With the ladders of success the organization has managed to wed the personal journey of self-discovery to the social journey of self-determination for the poor. Lee meant it when he told me that he was just a street hustler, interested only in himself. He could well have ended up homeless, in jail, or dead, but instead he has been able to carve out a new life for himself and his children. For him, the journey to self-discovery is an open-ended challenge involving both self-interest and the common good.

Reflecting on the approach and accomplishments of ADP, one is reminded of St. Paul, the ever-moving, hustling, working tent maker. Paul always wanted to pay his own way but also did not hesitate to confront authorities both civil and religious. Willing to confront, he quickly sought to move to reconciliation. "We must consider how to rouse one another to love and good works" (Heb 10:24). This is an apt reference for ADP's readiness to confront but also to rouse the opposition—the power structure—to join in the struggle for the poor.

The Catholic Campaign for Human Development and the Diocese of Springfield have supported ADP through its stages from organizing to economic development. The accomplishments are apparent—millions of dollars and thousands of housing units in accrued wealth and hundreds of jobs created with the potential for permanent career employment. ADP refuses to assist and maintain poor people as poor. The organization through its Ladders to Success constantly challenges itself and its members to think big and permanently break the cycle of poverty. While many organizations would have been content to remain on a lower rung, ADP keeps climbing. The linkage of community organization, housing, education, and economic development makes ADP a creative and successful example of social entrepreneurship and Catholic Social Teaching which uses business skills to accomplish a social justice mission. That's what the ladders are about. That is where the push comes from. ADP's manner of working provides us with a crystal-clear model of what Pope John Paul II discusses in *On Human Work:*

> The many proposals put forward by experts in Catholic Social Teaching and by the highest magisterium of the Church take on special significance: proposals for joint ownership of the means of work, sharing by the workers in the management and/or profits of business. . . . It is clear that recognition of the proper position of labor and the worker in the production process demands various adaptations in the sphere of the right to ownership of the means of production. (Pope John Paul II, *On Human Work*, 1981, p. 4.)

While the more timid among us might be uncomfortable with the somewhat confrontational style—the changed lives of Mary Lou, Ray, Lee, and indeed thousands of families should give us pause. Poor people being empowered is part of our Catholic Christian faith—a testament to human dignity and the power God has given to all of us. The working out of this power is a tiny, faint hint of the Kingdom Jesus spoke about. We all need to be reminded—as ADP reminds us—the gospel was meant to comfort the afflicted but it should also afflict the comfortable.

DISCUSSION QUESTIONS

1. The lack of affordable housing is causing low-income people in some areas to spend up to 50 percent of their income on housing or to move great distances from their work. Discuss this problem. What impact might it have on families? What portion of your income do you spend on mortgage or rent?
2. Discuss the strategic alliance ADP has formed with local groups and organizations. How important are unions in their work? What role do unions play in protecting workers?
3. What do you think about the type of worker-owned business ADP has set up? Do you think such an approach could work on a wider scale? What might be the advantages and disadvantages?
4. Discuss what you think of the "testing" that ADP did at Future-Works?

5. Are you offended by ADP's confrontational style? If so, why? In your own dealings with landlords, businesses, government bureaucracies, how do you handle situations where you run into a brick wall?
6. Discuss ADP's linkage of community organization, housing, jobs, education, and economic development. Why is this linkage so important? What impact does the linkage have on family life?

SUGGESTED PARISH ACTION

Through your Catholic Campaign for Human Development diocesan director, seek out a community organization doing work like ADP. Arrange for a CCHD "Journey to Justice" retreat weekend where members of your parish can dialogue with such a group and volunteer service, if appropriate, in support of their work or similar work. You might also encourage your diocese to invite the CCHD training program, "Education for Solidarity: Catholic Social Teaching and Economic Life."

CONTACTS

The Anti-Displacement Project, Inc.
57 School Street
Springfield, MA 01105
Tel. 413-739-7233
adp@javanet.com

For information on the "Journey to Justice" process, "Education for Solidarity training," or to contact your diocesan director, use the CCHD website: *www.usccb.org/cchd*

OPTIONAL FURTHER STUDY

Anti-Displacement Project, *FutureWorks: Roadblocks to Success* (Springfield, MA: ADP, March 2001).
Applied Research Center, *Common Goals: A Community Approach to Crime* (Oakland, CA: ARC, 2001), "The Anti-Displacement Project (ADP)," pp. 12–21.
Miriam Axel-Lute, "Don't Start Small: Tenants Organize for Ownership," *Shelterforce: Journal of Affordable Housing and Community Building* 117 (May/June 2001), pp. 8.
JoAnn Dilorenzo, "Owning Up to It," *City Limits* (July/August 2000), pp. 14–15, 33.
Dennis A. Jacobsen, *Doing Justice: Congregations and Community Organization* (Minneapolis: Fortress Press, 2001).
Thomas Massaro, S.J., *Living Justice: Catholic Social Teaching in Action* (Franklin, WI: Sheed and Ward, 2000), pp. 132–142.

6

A Parish Builds Neighborhood Peace: *Comunidad en Movimiento*

Los Angeles, California

SETTING: DOLORES MISSION—*PROYECTO PASTORAL*

In the early evening of October 8, 2000, a car sped down South Clarence Street in East Los Angeles and opened fire on a nineteen-year-old gang member who was washing his car. The young man was killed instantly and stray bullets took another, even younger life, Stephanie Raygoza. The ten-year-old girl was riding her scooter in front of her house. All along Clarence Street memorials to Stephanie appeared—not only little altars with photos, flowers, and candles, but also newly planted trees, new speed bumps, and new streetlights. Most importantly, a living memorial was constructed with the willingness of the community to come together and work for peace in their neighborhood.

For a community that had long suffered from violence and poverty, Stephanie's death became a rallying event—she became a symbol of new life and new hope for her neighbors.

> Whoever receives one child such as this in my name receives me; and whoever receives me, receives not me but the One who sent me (Mk 9:37).

She is even depicted as an angel in a large religious mural now hanging in Dolores Mission Parish Church. Father Mike Kennedy, the pastor, noted the sad irony that her parents were part of a parish group that had repeatedly asked for speed bumps to slow down traffic. The city

101

only acted after the killing of the two young people and when a large group of parents threatened a sit-in to block the street. Within days, the speed bumps and lights were installed. More importantly, residents, once too afraid to speak out against gang violence, now joined the parish effort to fight that violence. Nonetheless, the killings continue. There were twenty-four homicides in the area from January through May 2002!

How does this community find hope amidst so much suffering and death? So many families have lost children to gangs, drugs, and death. And yet, faith, hope, and even joy flourish on the streets surrounding Dolores Mission. The neighborhood's culture of death is being challenged.

> I have set before you life and death, the blessing and the curse. Choose life, then, that you and your descendants may live, by loving the LORD, your God, heeding his voice, and holding fast to him (Dt 30:19–20).

The focal point of that faith, hope, and challenge is Dolores Mission Church, one of the poorest parishes in the Archdiocese of Los Angeles. The little church which looks like an old California mission dropped into the sprawling East Los Angeles projects serves both as a peaceful sanctuary and defiant "Alamo" for the surrounding neighborhood. The church compound contains a homeless shelter, a food distribution program, and a daycare center. Across the street is the parish elementary school. Over the years, the Boyle Heights section was home to some of the largest public housing projects west of the Mississippi and is still a magnet for Mexican immigrants. Although the area is undergoing revitalization, the community is scarred by poverty, homelessness, domestic abuse, drugs, teen pregnancy, and gang violence. The majority of households are led by single mothers. Median family income is $20,000. Residents are 92 percent Latino. The area public schools are overcrowded and understaffed. Class size at the local high school and middle school is over forty-five students. Unemployment is high, especially because of language and citizenship barriers. With revitalization, the area's living arrangement has recently been greatly altered by the demolition of the 685 units of the Aliso Village Project. This has displaced many families and even thrown into question the balance of power among gangs.

While the statistics tell the all-too-common tale of urban decay, violence, and the plight of new immigrants, there is something unique about the parish. Dolores Mission provides a very different model of church but one which fits well with its Latino community. The Jesuit-run parish puts great emphasis on three points: an Ignatian approach to spiritual life; empowering the laity; and social justice concerns. This entails working from the ground up—*desde la base*. The forum for this approach—listening to and reflecting on people's faith in daily life—are the small bible reflection groups, *comunidades eclesiales de base* (Christian base communities), which are the core of parish faith and action.

On a Tuesday night, Rita, one of the mothers and a parish community organizer, took me into one of the projects to the small but comfortable living room of Esperanza, a long-time parish leader, who was hosting this week's bible reflection/prayer meeting. Ten women members of the "Holy Trinity" group were present for their regular meeting. The meetings follow a simple pattern. The host welcomes the group, a hymn is sung, and then a scripture passage is read. After the reading, a few minutes are spent in silent reflection, and then the group shares "what we have seen and heard." How does the passage touch our daily lives? What does it say to our families, marriages, our failures and hopes? What does it say to our communion in the Body of Christ? To our communion in the struggle to overcome the violence around us and build a better community?

The gospel text that night was John 20:19–31, Jesus' post-Resurrection appearance to his followers hiding in fear, afraid to go out. Jesus' "Peace be with you . . ." really spoke to the women—Esperanza V., Lupe, Rosa, Ana, Rita, Maria, Esperanzita, Blanca, and Esperanza R. are often afraid to go out, even to church or school. In their own everyday struggles, they were able to relate intimately to Thomas and his doubts. "Have you come to believe because you have seen me? Blessed are those who have not seen and have believed." After some quiet minutes, papers were handed around with questions: Give an example when you doubted God. What was happening in your life at that time? Give an example when God brought life out of death in your experience; in your community? Each woman carefully wrote down her reflections and, after all had enough time, each one shared her thoughts.

The first to speak told of how desperate and embarrassed she was to learn that her own son had become a gang member and was involved in drugs and shootings. The "despair was heavy." She was even ashamed to go to Mass. However, she sought out Father Greg Boyle, at that time pastor at Dolores Mission. The priest supported her and her son through that dark period. Another woman described her long marriage to an alcoholic husband and her struggle to raise eight children. She said she could not have done it without the support of the community of Dolores Mission. A third participant told of the recent shooting of a teen-aged boy in the local recreation center right next to her house. Gang members shot the boy in front of 100 watching kids and parents. Young people had gone to watch a girls' basketball tournament but found themselves in a war zone. A recent arrival from Mexico recounted the cruel poverty and illness her family members are suffering as migrant workers trying to free themselves from a hopeless situation. The last woman to speak said that her two brothers had been murdered in the gang violence. She remembered the day her second brother was shot. She had given up on life, but her mother knelt and prayed, "This is not God's justice. God will do His job." The woman said that at that time she simply hadn't understood her mother's prayer and doubted God's justice. But gradually with the help of Father Mike and the people of Dolores Mission, her faith returned. For me, it was fascinating to watch how the women were able to identify with each other's sufferings and doubts. But the reflection and reaction never moved to self-pity or fatalism. Rather joy, healing, new direction, and new action evolved from the shared reflection. Their stories were a contemporary retelling of the paschal mystery of Christ: somehow they were able to see through the death to new life.

> The community does not close in on itself, but rather integrates families of grandparents, parents, sisters, and brothers. It promotes strong interpersonal relationships based on faith, love, and unity. Members share their daily lives, their basic problems, their joys, and their struggles. All feel welcomed there—integrated and co-responsible—with a fundamental equality, even if there is a diversity of function. Members of the community demonstrate a mutual, profound, caring, loving, and committed partnership that brings them together in solidarity. (U.S. Bishops, *Communion and Mission: A Guide for Bishops and Pastoral Leaders on Small Church Communities*, 1995, p. 7.)

Gradually, the women moved to concrete action for justice in their efforts for safe streets. Establishing the links between personal experiences, healing faith, and community action is clearly the key to the integral faith practiced at Dolores Mission.

The meeting ended as apparently they always do, with a *convivencia*. The word means a "get-together" or "sharing of life" but here it meant a small meal or snack which the women prepare and share. This sharing of life and faith plays a big role in the community. The parish, the Eucharistic community, is fed by the small prayer meeting groups and flows out into outreach programs and schools.

This *convivencia* is incarnated in what is called *Proyecto Pastoral*. This parish-based non-profit organization, directed by Leonora Lozano-Ramirez, has six components, each of which embodies key themes in Catholic Social Teaching—dignity of the person and human rights, family life, participation, solidarity, social or structural sin, rights of immigrants, and the option for the poor. Proyecto Pastoral has the following components:

- *Jobs for a Future and Homeboy Industries* is a job referral and placement center for at-risk, gang-impacted youth. The Jobs for a Future component includes job training, youth counseling, and tattoo removal. It provides one of the only places where youth can relate across gang lines. The Homeboy Industry component is a start-up economic development program providing business opportunities for young people.
- *Guadaloupe Homeless Project* shelters up to sixty men every night and offers meals and showers as well as access to social, medical, and mental health services, and job and citizenship counseling. Residents are responsible for the facility and assist with weekly food distribution to the whole community.
- *Women's Cooperative Childcare Center* provides daycare and preschool to children on a year-round basis. In 2001, a new facility was opened called the *Centro de Alegria* which provides licensed professional daycare for over fifty children, ages eighteen months to five years. The center also serves as a training site for mothers working toward their Early Childhood Education certificates through East Los Angeles Community College.
- *Impacto-Leadership Challenge* is an after-school tutoring program that offers youth ages 7–16 computer classes, field trips, counseling, and homework assistance as well as leadership development work with parents and teachers.
- *Dolores Mission Alternative School* is an alternative high school for youth who because of gang affiliation, teen pregnancy, or other issues cannot attend regular high school. The school has over forty students and boasts successful retention and college entrance rates.

Our primary concern in this case study is *Comunidad en Movimiento* (Community in Action), the organizing component of Proyecto Pastoral. This community organization effort, supported by the Catholic Campaign for Human Development and the Archdiocese of Los Angeles, promotes outreach in the wider community and fosters linkage among the various efforts of Proyecto Pastoral.

Communidad en Movimiento was begun in 1996. Residents in the area were concerned about the new welfare and immigration reform laws.

In its history, America has experienced many immigrations as waves of men and women came to its various regions in the hope of a better future. The phenomenon continues even today especially with many people and families from Latin American countries who have moved to the northern parts of the continent to the point where in some cases they constitute a substantial part of the population. They often bring with them a cultural and religious heritage which is rich in Christian elements.

The Church . . . is committed to spare no effort in developing her own pastoral strategy among these immigrant people in order to help them settle in their new land and to foster a welcoming attitude among the local population in the belief that a mutual openness will bring enrichment to all. (John Paul II, *Ecclesia in America*, no. 65.)

Building on all the components of Proyecto Pastoral, the community mobilized itself around the most pressing concerns: housing, human rights, citizenship, and violence in the area. The organizing effort serves over 500 families with leadership development, health workshops, citizenship classes, and legal support through the naturalization process. An important feature is the annual women's conference which provides leadership training for local women in dealing with health issues, family life, domestic abuse, creative arts, and career opportunities. *Comunidad en Movimiento* is headed by Consuelo Valdez, a dynamic organizer who clearly has the talent for finding and empowering women leaders from the community. Claudia Martinon and Rita Chairez are the lead organizers; they work with parish organizer, Mario Fuentes, and each in turn works with local leaders—usually women.

The most important dynamic in this organizing process is the fact that leadership, issues, and implementation steps all emerge from the base community prayer groups. Discipleship and organization emerge from the experience and prayers of the local community.

Another important dynamic is the leadership role assumed by women—mothers, grandmothers, and aunts who serve as the community's conveyors and interpreters of reality. It is true that some men have come forth and are becoming more involved in the base communities. But for the most part, the men seem willing to support the leadership role the women have taken in community organizing.

Commitment and discipleship, suffering and hope, sin and grace are reflected through the women leaders. Theologian Orlando Espin beautifully captures this filtering role: "Latina women are our families' interpreters of

Particular attention needs to be given to the vocation of women. . . . Without this contribution, we would miss the enrichment which only the "feminine genius" can bring to the life of the Church and society. (John Paul II, *Ecclesia in America*, 1999, no. 45.)

the biblical message and of the heart and mind of God, the teachers of ethics and the leaders of our prayers, our families' living sacraments of God and the sacred. Life and their own observations (shared and affirmed by other women) have taught them wisdom. Reflection and prayer inspired them to trust in the ultimate goodness of God and human life. Their own suffering has been their best schooling." Espin could well have been describing the women of Dolores Mission.

After careful observation and long suffering, *Comunidad en Movimiento* has zeroed in on the problem of violence in the community. "The killings have to stop!" An organizing effort involving leadership training, community education, collection and dissemination of accurate information and statistics now began to focus squarely on safe streets for children, reducing gang impact, and cajoling the Los Angeles Police Department (LAPD) into more serious involvement with the community.

SAFE PASSAGE AND COMMUNITY SAFETY

Over the course of the last few years, the mothers of Dolores Mission have seen too many of their children gunned down on their streets. Their pastor Father Mike Kennedy has listened to and prayed with too many young people in Central Juvenile Hall in Los Angeles. Dead kids and boys facing serious prison time have motivated a deep parish-wide commitment to create options for young people and build peace in the community.

On a Thursday afternoon, not long after the young man was murdered in the neighborhood recreation center, Claudia, a young mother and one of the project's organizers, asked me to join her *Camino Seguro* (Safe Passage) group for their daily duty patrolling the streets. The women and a few men wear green jackets or T-shirts, clearly identifying them as "Safe Passage" volunteers. Because of the lack of police presence on their streets, especially around schools, the parents, with direction and training from *Comunidad en Movimiento*, have taken on the task of ensuring the safety of their children. Ana, Esperanza, and Carmen moved through the whole neighborhood, checking in with other parents, Raphael, Bertha, Margarita, and Rosa, who were strategically placed on certain corners near Dolores Mission School, Second Street School, and Utah Street School. The parents coordinate their efforts and have fixed schedules for covering the hours when children are going to school and when they are returning home in the afternoon. When problems arise, they communicate by walkie-talkie. It was amazing to look up and down the long flat neighborhood streets and see two adults in green jackets—like beacons of hope on every corner! The parents receive bare-bones training in what to look out for—violent behavior, drug dealers, or simply speeding cars. They also know the location of "safe houses"—the church, schools, or private homes where they can quickly go for help. Most importantly, neighborhood kids, young and old, know they can trust Claudia, Esperanza, Raphael, and the rest of the "green team."

In the face of violence, parents, especially mothers, have become models of peace for their children. Increasingly more men are joining the Safe Passage teams. *Camino Seguro* now has over fifty parents who regularly volunteer their time. This has been *Comunidad en Movimiento's* major thrust in taking leadership against violence in the community. But Lupe, Rita, Esperanza, Maria, Claudia, and Raphael all agree that it does not solve the wider problem. Father Kennedy, who also participates in a Safe Passage team and regular "peace walks," pointed out that "we can't assume the role of the police." His fellow Jesuit Father Greg Boyle told a local newspaper, "We need the palpable presence of the police in order to have authentic peace."

The Safe Passage program thrives and serves a number of constructive purposes, but the death of little Stephanie catapulted the community to the next steps in organizing against violence. These parents who have literally put their own lives on the line in defense of their children realized more was needed. *Comunidad en Movimiento* mobilized for action.

After the shooting of the two young people on Clarence Street, gang violence and drugs became everyone's priority. A march was immediately organized. Residents led off with a large banner, "Homies Stop the Violence—Your Presence Puts Us in Danger." Lupe led the charge for the speed bumps and better lighting: "If by Friday we don't have a response from the councilman, we will organize a protest with civil disobedience and close the street with a chain of human bodies." She added, "We want the police to do their job; we are tired of all the violence." The voice of the people was heard, at least, in the short run. Police presence was beefed up—even horse and bike patrols were added. Speed bumps and new lights were installed and a drug alley was sealed off. But according to residents, the police presence quickly dwindled. A more strategic and long-term plan was needed. *Comunidad en Movimiento* took up the challenge.

To respond to the complex questions of violence, drugs, and the appalling lack of resources for youth and families, residents knew they had to engage the LAPD and city officials. *Comunidad en Movimiento* recruited and trained twenty-five leaders from the parish. The training included conducting over 500 one-on-one interviews with local residents to carefully identify concerns. The leaders participated in several research meetings with elected officials, the housing authority, police department, and community-based organizations.

> It is the duty of the laity—without idly waiting for norms and precepts from others—by their free planning and initiative to permeate not only (people's) customs and mentality, but also the laws and structures of the civil community with a Christian sense of life. (Pope Paul VI, *On the Development of Peoples*, 1967, no. 8.)

Community leaders traveled to Chicago and San Diego to learn about the successful community policing models implemented in those cities. Community policing is an innovative nationwide initiative which aligns police practice more closely with the needs of the local community. To learn more about this initiative, local leaders received instruction from the U.S. Department of Justice's National Institute of Justice.

The whole learning process was a liberating experience for the community leaders. The overwhelming majority of local residents interviewed identified gang violence and drugs as major concerns. Research also indicated that current police work is not keeping pace with shifting demographics and the culture of the community. Most importantly, interviews revealed a deep mistrust of police on the part of residents. The mistrust too often translates to apathy and has been a major obstacle to building fruitful relations with the police.

The leaders learned a great deal visiting community policing projects. They were able to see how many people shared their concerns, both in Los Angeles and around the country. They returned hoping to develop plans in full partnership with the LAPD. It is significant that the women chose not to use the national name of "community policing" for what they were trying to accomplish. They knew they were asking the city of Los Angeles to experiment with them. They wanted a "pilot" which would try some new policing approaches but tailored to their needs. They named their approach the "Dolores Mission Community Safety Pilot Project." The primary goal of the pilot is to create policies and structures involving police and community, that would prevent, or at least reduce, violent, gang-related crimes.

The organization effort, research, and commitment came to a head on November 10, 2001, with a large community action meeting. *Communidad en Movimiento* turned out over 500 people. With the aid of Cardinal Mahony and Bishop Zavala, the community received the support of the mayor's office as well as commitments from the police chief and their city council member. Maria Elena, a young single mother prepared by months of research and study, chaired and ran the meeting. Building on their faith-based organizing skills, the women presented the problems, provided the data, and gently but firmly demanded a commitment from city authorities to work with them against violence. During their presentation, they used charts, statistical information, and detailed maps to help make their case for the project. Leticia stated, "Developing and implementing this program has tremendous significance for us as residents. We have been experiencing a form of terrorism for years—gang violence and open drug dealings—and we want to put a stop to it."

The careful and skillful planning and research done by the volunteer leaders was impressive—even to experts in the field of community policing. Arthur Jones and Robin Wiseman of the Institute for International Human Rights Law and Policy wrote, "Resident activism, diligent research, and a year of inspired planning recently produced a user-friendly program of community policing" (*Daily News,* December 9, 2001). At the community action meeting, the leaders presented a set of principles designed to restructure how police in their neighborhood are assigned and promoted and how they interact with the local community.

The long range plan for the pilot was well-designed and built on the following principles: 1) A commitment from the police department and city officials to develop the pilot with residents and implement the program by July 1, 2002; 2) A one-year commitment from police and city and the community to meet regularly and work through implementation; 3) Problem-solving police methods not limited to reacting to 911 calls but rather focused on crime prevention; 4) Around-the-clock presence of two police officers in order to develop sound community relations; 5) Assignment of Spanish-speaking officers who want to work with this kind of pilot program; 6) Permanent assignment of officers for at least one year with career incentives to maintain this presence in the community so mutual trust can be built; 7) Police officer promotion and incentives based on effective local community work; 8) Flexible work hours so officers are able to attend community events and meetings; 9) Creation of a mechanism for evaluation and accountability to monitor the pilot. This includes monthly "beat meetings" with police officers.

Integral to the plan was close collaboration among all the relevant city agencies—parks and recreation, social services, education, job training, and even graffiti removal. *Communidad en Movimiento* was very cognizant that crime and violence in their community was not simply a matter of police presence, important as that is. They wanted to provide alternative opportunities to the gang culture—recreation, education, and jobs. The pilot aims for prevention, counseling, and rehabilitation.

> As it engages in social teaching, the Church embraces the quest for justice as an eminently religious task. Persons engaged in this endeavor must be involved with, informed by, and increasingly led by those who know from experience the paradoxical blessings of poverty, prejudice, and unfairness (Mt 5:3). Accordingly, we urge Hispanics to increase their role in social action, and non-Hispanics increasingly to seek out Hispanics in a true partnership. (U.S. Catholic Bishops, *The Hispanic Presence: Challenge and Commitment*, 1983, III, L.)

In spite of all the violence Dolores Mission mothers had suffered, they were not going to give up on their children. Lupe R. said "what we were proposing was not always popular but it was empowering. We're making a change for our children."

Of course, the devil was in the details, and, in spite of the initial rush to support, the police department and city officials dragged their feet in implementing the pilot project. The women of Dolores Mission, however, did not slow down. Instead they zeroed in on the tepid response from the police and city officials—no anonymous "cold" phone line; failure of police to realign assignments in spite of promises; no assistance around schools. The police made a commitment but did not live up to its end of the bargain.

At a leaders' meeting in April 2002, Mario Fuentes, organizer at Dolores Mission, discussed with the women the two kinds of power used in city political discourse—money and people. Of course, it was the latter which emboldened the women of Dolores Mission. Mario pointed out the example of Jesus and how he tried to involve everyone—the poor, the non-poor, and the authorities. "We need the bottom-up effort, *desde la base*, but how do we get the authorities to listen to this voice from below and meet us halfway?" This started the group on a discussion of *"pasos concretos"*—concrete steps. Maria Elena, Berta, Xochitl, Rosa, and Lidia were adamant, "We have to make it clear we are not playing. Our children are being killed." The group agreed to call for another large community assembly, this time with the mayor and the new acting police chief present. Each woman left the meeting with a commitment to bring twenty-five people to the assembly. Out of apparent death, the women of Dolores Mission sought to bring life.

Once again, *Comunidad en Movimiento's* energizing the community paid off. After another immense organizing effort, 500 people packed into the Dolores Mission schoolyard on May 15, 2002. The women leaders led the charge with Los Angeles Mayor Hahn and the new acting police chief present. "We are here today because we care about our community and because we care about the safety of all families." A *Los Angeles Times* editorial (5/3/02) strongly backed the pilot: "How many more children will young gangsters murder before adults with the power to change this city forcefully intervene?" This time the mayor heard the plea as did the local police commander and new acting chief. They announced the implementation of the Dolores Mission Community Safety Pilot Project beginning July 1, 2002. The anonymous phone line for reporting crimes was installed and police presence was increased in the Dolores Mission area. Regular meetings were set up between police and community leaders. The women in the green shirts are still patrolling their own streets, but they are a little less afraid. The long struggle paid off.

The women of Dolores Mission have worked hard to link constructive elements in their neighborhoods to police and other city agencies. This is the kind of partnership they deserve to see work. It might also be a model deserving of replication. *The Los Angeles Times* (May 25, 2002) called for just that: "Church bells peeled last week when L.A. Mayor James K. Hahn and interim LAPD Chief Martin Pomeroy agreed to a yearlong experiment teaming police with Boyle Heights residents. . . . The mothers of Boyle Heights are battling the murderers among them as best they can. We commend the mayor for watching their backs—and urge him to name a leader or task force to work with other neighborhoods too."

The women did not give up. They continue to live out Jesus' paschal mystery on the streets of Boyle Heights in East Los Angeles—both in prayer and action. The Archdiocese of Los Angeles acknowledged the group's accomplishments when Cardinal Mahony awarded *Comunidad en Movimiento* and Dolores Mission the 2001 Empowerment Award. He said, "Dolores Mission—through *Comunidad en Movimiento* and *Proyecto Pastoral*—demonstrates the potential of our parishes to be agents of transformation. They not only preach the Good News of the Gospel . . . they live it out each and every day." The women of *Comunidad en Movimiento* beamed with pride.

ACTIVITIES AND ACCOMPLISHMENTS

The various components of *Proyecto Pastoral* at Dolores Mission have made significant contributions to job creation and education for youth-at-risk, childcare, women's leadership training, immigrants, and the homeless.

Comunidad en Movimiento, the community organizing component, with funding assistance from the Catholic Campaign for Human Development, has greatly added to the overall parish effort and in a sense serves to integrate the project components. Begun only in 1996, its major accomplishment has been the empowerment of local women leaders. Other significant accomplishments include:

- Recruitment and training of more than fifty parents in the neighborhood Safe Passage—*Camino Seguro*—campaign
- Organization and implementation of the annual United Women's Conference—*Conferencia de Mujeres Unidas*—with over 200 participants each year
- Assistance with and preparation for naturalization of over 200 new U.S. citizens
- Organization of peace walks and press conferences to raise awareness of the impact of gang violence
- Research, planning, and organization with LAPD of the Community Safety Pilot Project. Program was implemented by Mayor Hahn and LAPD on July 1, 2002

EVALUATION/IMPACT

The impact of this community organizing effort should be assessed in light of its parish and faith base. *Comunidad en Movimiento* grows directly out of the prayer and reflection of the small "basic Christian communities" but has impact far beyond those groups. Every housing project, every local community organization, and every school in the Boyle Heights, East Los Angeles area has been impacted by this effort, especially the organizing around gang violence and children's safety. As Richard Wood, an expert in community policing has written, "With the right partners from LAPD and the city, this pilot project might not only make a difference in Boyle Heights, it may offer a model for broader efforts to reclaim neighborhoods and rebuild police legitimacy throughout Los Angeles."

REFLECTION

A writer asked Father Mike Kennedy, "Are the gangs like those seen on television and in the movies?" He quickly replied: "Much worse. The neighborhood is soaked in blood. A lot of mothers of the parish have lost their sons on these streets." The people of Dolores Mission live with violence and death, but what is truly miraculous is that they don't succumb to that culture of death. They don't lose heart. Particularly, the women refuse to give up the struggle for safe streets and a better way of life for their children. The miracle is that the struggle is a joyful one. Many years ago the French writer Leon Bloy told us that "joy is the most infallible sign of the presence of God." That joyful presence animates Dolores Mission—even in the face of death. That joyful presence compels the women to speak "truth to power"—whether gang leader or police chief. That joyful presence molds family and community, hope and unity. Ana, a young mother, said, "Whatever happens, we are united. . . . My community is my family and I have to fight for it."

Where does such spunk come from? Upon reflection, it is clear that the long hours put into the Safe Passage Project and the tedious year-long planning and research involved in the Community Safety Pilot Project as well as the other activities of *Comunidad en Movimiento* and *Proyecto Pastoral* are dependent on a deep faith commitment.

Father Kennedy's "guided meditations" are a key to this intimate linkage of spirituality and the quest for social justice. The Ignatian "meditations," which form the nucleus of the basic communities as well as parish preaching, invite parishioners right into the middle of the gospel scenes—the places, the people, the faith. The scenes, in turn, penetrate the life of their own community—the sufferings, the hopes, and the joys. Looking with the eyes of Jesus stretches the imagination and forces new ways of seeing life's problems and potentials. This approach provides a framework that beats back despair and death and keeps faith and hope alive. This prophetic model of Church could be of value to all of us, no matter what our circumstances. In 1995, the U.S. Bishops' Committee on Hispanic Affairs discussed this approach.

> Small church communities critically investigate the root causes of the idols of death, which are the obstacles to God's plan. They also interpret the signs of the times from the view of the mission of Jesus. Therefore, when small communities discuss, plan, and focus on what direction to take, they begin and end with their commitment to the task of the coming reign of God. In this way, these church communities become faithful to Christ's mission by refusing to give idols of death a place in history. As prophetic communities, they confront sin as an annihilation of communion with God and with one another. (*Communion and Mission: A Guide for Bishops and Pastoral Leaders on Small Church Communities*, March 1995, p. 9.)

This paragraph of the Bishops neatly summarizes the lived faith of Dolores Mission. That faith is a form of resistance to the wider culture of conflict, consumerism, individualism, and death. The Safe Passage Project and the Community Safety Pilot Project are the parish's way of resisting the idols of death.

Their solidarity, empowerment, creative decisions, and actions emerge directly from a shared prayer life. In *Eyes on the Cross: A Guide for Contemplation*, Father Kennedy meditates with the community on the Safe Passage Project. His reflection "Walking With" describes an October afternoon as the pastor was taking his turn on the Safe Passage team with parish women. Suddenly shots rang out in front of the church and another stray bullet did its damage. The parish grammar school was letting out and mothers were picking up children. The police let Father Mike through to comfort the bleeding boy who kept repeating, "I don't want to die, I don't want to die." The ambulance came and all that was left of the shooting was the stained street. The community was trying to protect its children and here was one with a bullet in his neck. "But our walking, our accompanying children on our streets, is a small sign that our God is a God who desires life not death." Kennedy's meditation speaks through Mary as she faces her son's arrest and execution, but the scenes fade in and out of the streets of East Los Angeles.

> i came closer/to jesus
> the soldiers moved away
> i put my hand
> on the bloody shoulder
> of my son/my son
> my hand wet with blood
> blood not being shed in vain
> but would give strength/hope
> to all those who follow him
> who struggle/to build a better world
> (Michael Kennedy, *Eyes on the Cross:*
> *A Guide for Contemplation.*)

When Maria Elena, Ana, Rita, and Claudia, and the other women worked on the Community Safety Pilot, they were confronted with a real Calvary moment. Some people saw them as "traitors;" others feared for their well-being, predicting gang retaliation. Others ridiculed them saying that they would not be taken seriously. But like Mary they didn't run away. Rita told me she was afraid but prayed, "OK, God, I leave it in your hands. I don't want my kids dead in the street. Either I run or I stay and fight." With the support of Dolores Mission and *Comunidad en Movimiento*, she stayed, and so did the other mothers.

Let us stop and reflect prayerfully on the work of *Comunidad en Movimiento*. A group of mainly Mexican immigrant women volunteers have painstakingly researched and organized a sound, professional approach to community safety. Moreover, they are out on the street everyday, patrolling and trying to protect their children. How many of us could or would take on that responsibility?

> The church's social doctrine also makes possible a clearer apprecia-
> tion of the gravity of the "social sins which cry to heaven because
> they generate violence, disrupt peace and harmony between com-
> munities." . . . Among these must be mentioned: "the drug trade . . .
> corruption . . . the terror of violence . . . racial discrimination, in-
> equality between social groups. . . ." (John Paul II, *Ecclesia in Amer-
> ica*, no. 56.)

The Dolores Mission Community Safety Pilot Project attacks a glaring
and painful social sin—the alienation and isolation of young people
which results from a lack of resources and options. The pilot is a start
down the path to create alternatives. It does so by putting into action the
Catholic social principles concerning family, participation, solidarity, and
the preferential option for the poor. These principles, in many ways,
summarize the methods and goals of Dolores Mission and *Comunidad en
Movimiento*.

> The human person is not only sacred, but social. We realize our dig-
> nity and rights in relationship with others, in community. . . . The fam-
> ily has major contributions to make in addressing questions of social
> justice. It is where we learn and act on our values. . . . (U.S. Catholic
> Bishops, *A Century of Social Teaching*, p. 5.)

The women of Dolores Mission adamantly refused "to give the idols of
death a place in history." Their respect for the dignity of the human person, for family and community, pervades all that they do—both in prayer
and action. They never give up on their children. The Catholic Campaign
for Human Development has supported this organizing initiative because
it is clear that all of the good works, for the poor, the homeless, education,
economic development, and jobs, are dependent on a safe community
and the reversal of violence. Human development cannot happen without
a sense of peace and security.

What a lesson for all of us, the "spunk" and "joy" of these courageous
women grows from their prayer life, their "healing meditations," the
family-like solidarity found in base communities and parish-based eucharistic unity. "Go in peace" at the end of Mass at Dolores Mission is
loaded with meaning. The joy that comes from solidarity, in the midst of

struggle, continues to be "the most infallible sign of the presence of God" and indeed, a most "credible sign of Christ alive."

DISCUSSION QUESTIONS

1. Have you or someone close to you (or your parish) lost a young person to gang violence or drug abuse? What impact did that loss have on family and parish?
2. What do you think pushes young people to drugs and gangs? Does your neighborhood have gang problems or drug problems? What factors make a neighborhood or area more prone to gangs?
3. Discuss what you think about the intimate links between spiritual life and the quest for social justice at Dolores Mission. What do you think about the parish meditations? Does that model of church have any lessons for the average Catholic parish?
4. Talk about the leadership role played by the Catholic women in East Los Angeles. Why and how were they empowered? How does their role compare to that of women in your parish?
5. What do you think of police service in your area? What would you suggest to improve it? Do you see the police on your street? Do you feel comfortable talking to the police officers in your neighborhood? Do you get the opportunity to speak with them? To the local police commander? To your city's police chief? Why are you comfortable or uncomfortable?
6. Have you lived through a situation where you experienced both suffering and joy? What caused the suffering? Where did the joy come from? What part did family, participation, and solidarity play?
7. In what ways are you and your parish walled off from the lives of the poor, the lonely, or the marginalized? In what ways are you connected to those suffering or alone?

SUGGESTED PARISH ACTION

To better understand the Dolores Mission *Comunidad en Movimiento* approach to prayer and action for social justice, meditate on and discuss Michael Kennedy's *The Jesus Meditations*. The book comes with a CD with Martin Sheen reading the reflections. After these reflections, contact your diocesan CCHD director for information on how your parish might establish a "twinning" relationship with a parish in your area facing problems similar to Dolores Mission. How might you learn from their struggles and perhaps offer some assistance?

CONTACTS

Proyecto Pastoral at Dolores Mission
Comunidad en Movimiento
135 North Mission Road
Los Angeles, CA 90033
Tel. 323-881-0014

To contact your CCHD diocesan director, use CCHD website: *www. usccb.org/cchd*

OPTIONAL FURTHER STUDY

Orlando O. Espin and Miguel H. Diaz, eds., *From the Heart of the People: Latino/a Explorations in Catholic Systematic Theology* (Maryknoll, NY: Orbis Books, 1999). See especially Espin, "An Exploration into the Theology of Grace and Sin," pp. 121–152.

Arthur A. Jones and Robin Wiseman, "Community Policing Must Be Restored," *Daily News* (Los Angeles), *Viewpoint,* December 9, 2001.

James Thomas Keane and Richard L. Wood, *Reclaiming our Neighborhood: The Dolores Mission Community Safety Project* (Los Angeles: National Institute of Justice, May 2002).

Michael Kennedy, S.J., *Eyes on the Cross* (New York: Crossroad, 1999). See especially, "Walking With," pp. 173–181.

——, *Eyes on Jesus* (New York: Crossroad, 1999).

—— with Martin Sheen, *The Jesus Meditations* (New York: Crossroad, 2002).

Thomas Massaro, S.J., *Living Justice: Catholic Social Teaching in Action* (Franklin, WI: 2000), pp. 25–51; 119–127; 158–163; 211–214.

U.S. Bishops' Committee on Hispanic Affairs, *Communion and Mission: A Guide for Bishops and Pastoral Leaders on Small Church Communities* (Washington, DC: USCC, 1995).

Appendix 1

Poverty USA: The State of Poverty in America

- In America's forgotten state, 34 million people live in poverty, which is 12.5 percent of the population. *(U.S. Census Bureau, 2000 Supplementary Survey)*
- Overall, the poverty rate for all U.S. children (under 18) is 16.3 percent or nearly 12 million and children still represent the largest population group living in poverty. *(U.S. Census Bureau Survey 2000, Issued September 2002)*
- The 2002 official poverty guideline for a family of four, as defined by the U.S. Department of Health and Human Services, was $18,100. A 2002 poll revealed that most Americans believe it takes nearly $35,000 annually for a family of four to make ends meet. *("Poverty Pulse" by Catholic Campaign for Human Development, November 2002)*
- The average American, now age 20, has about a 60 percent chance of spending at least one year living in poverty at some point in the future. By age 35, about 31 percent of the U.S. population will have experienced a year in poverty. By age 65, the figure rises to 51 percent, and by age 85, it exceeds 66 percent. ("The Likelihood of Poverty across the American Adult Life Span" by Mark R. Rank and Thomas A. Hirschl, *Social Work*, May 1999)
- One in 10 families, one in eight Americans, and one in six children in the United States lives in poverty. *(U.S. Census Bureau, Current Population Survey, September 2002)*

THE FACE OF POVERTY IN AMERICA

Poverty touches all ethnicities and races, ages and family types, with minorities experiencing much higher poverty rates than whites. African-Americans have a poverty rate of 22.5 percent while American Indians and Alaska Natives have a 24.5 percent poverty rate, more than three times the rate of whites, whose poverty rate is 7.8 percent; 21.4 percent of Hispanics are poor; 10.2 percent of Asians and Pacific Islanders are poor. *(U.S. Census Bureau, Current Population Survey, September 2002)*

Over 55 percent of children under 18, living in female-headed households, lived below the poverty level in 2000. *(U.S. Census Bureau, Current Population Survey, March 2001)*

The Working Poor

- Twenty-nine percent of working families in the United States with one to three children under age 12 do not earn enough income to afford basic necessities like food, housing, health care, and childcare. *(Economic Policy Institute, 2001)*
- Nearly 40 percent of America's poor over the age of 16 worked either part-time or full-time in 2001—yet could not earn enough to satisfy their basic needs.
- Three out of four children in poverty lived with a family member who worked at least part-time. And one out of every three children in poverty lived with someone who worked full-time, year round. *(U.S. Census Bureau, 2002 Supplementary Survey)*
- A single parent of two young children working full-time in a minimum wage job for a year would make $10,712 before taxes—more than $4,300 below the poverty line. *(U.S. Census Bureau, Current Population Survey, March 2001)*

Top 10 States with Highest Poverty Rate, 2000–2001

State % People below Poverty Level	
1. New Mexico	17.7%
2. Mississippi	17.1%
3. Arkansas	17.1%
4. District of Columbia	16.7%
5. Louisiana	16.7%
6. West Virginia	15.6%
7. Texas	15.2%
8. Oklahoma	15.0%
9. Alabama	14.6%
10. New York	14.0%

U.S. Census Bureau, Current Population Survey, 2002

**The Poverty Threshold: How the Government
Defines Poverty in America**

To arrive at the *poverty threshold*, the amount at which a person or family
has enough money for minimal nutritional subsistence and basic living
costs, government analysts at the Social Security Administration started
with the U.S. Department of Agriculture's least expensive plan for nutritional subsistence, called the "Economy Food Plan." This amount they arrived at was multiplied by three to allow for expenses other than food,
and the resulting amount was multiplied by the number of persons in a
family to produce a sliding threshold of poverty based on family size. For
a family of four, the poverty threshold in 1963 was $2,100; in 2002 it was
$18,100. The *poverty rate* measures the proportion of a population whose
cash income is below this amount. (*From research by Paul Sullins, Life Cycle
Institute, The Catholic University of America*)

Excerpts from CCHD website: *www.usccb.org/cchd/povertyusa*

Appendix 2

Excerpts from Being Neighbor: The Catechism and Social Justice

DIGNITY OF THE HUMAN PERSON

"Created in the image of the one God and equally endowed with rational souls, all . . . have the same nature and the same origin. Redeemed by the sacrifice of Christ, all are called to participate in the same divine beatitude: all therefore enjoy equal dignity" (CCC, no. 1934).

COMMUNITY AND THE COMMON GOOD

". . . The common good requires the *social well-being* and *development* of the group itself. Development is the epitome of all social duties. Certainly, it is the proper function of authority to arbitrate, in the name of the common good, between various particular interests; but it should make accessible to each what is needed to lead a truly human life: food, clothing, health, work, education and culture, suitable information, the right to establish a family, and so on"[1] (CCC, no. 1908).

RIGHTS AND RESPONSIBILITIES

"Man is himself the author, center, and goal of all economic and social life. The decisive point of the social question is that goods created by God for everyone should in fact reach everyone in accordance with justice and with the help of charity" (CCC, no. 2459).

OPTION FOR AND WITH THE POOR

"'Not to enable the poor to share in our goods is to steal from them and deprive them of life. The goods we possess are not ours, but theirs.'[2] 'The demands of justice must be satisfied first of all; that which is already due in justice is not to be offered as a gift of charity.'[3]

> When we attend to the needs of those in want, we give them what is theirs, not ours. More than performing works of mercy, we are paying a debt of justice"[4] (CCC, no. 2446).

DIGNITY OF WORK

"Everyone should be able to draw from work the means of providing for his life and that of his family, and of serving the human community" (CCC, no. 2428).

SOLIDARITY

"Various causes of a religious, political, economic, and financial nature today give 'the social question a worldwide dimension.'[5] There must be solidarity among nations which are already politically interdependent. It is even more essential when it is a question of dismantling the 'perverse mechanisms' that impede the development of the less advanced countries.[6] In place of abusive if not usurious financial systems, iniquitous commercial relations among nations, and the arms race, there must be substituted a common effort to mobilize resources toward objectives of moral, cultural, and economic development, 'redefining the priorities and hierarchies of values'"[7] (CCC, no. 2438).

CARE FOR GODS' CREATION

"*Each creature possesses its own particular goodness and perfection.* For each one of the works of the 'six days' it is said: 'And God saw that it was good.' 'By the very nature of creation, material being is endowed with its own stability, truth, and excellence, its own order and laws.'[8] Each of these various creatures, willed in its own being, reflects in its own way a ray of God's infinite wisdom and goodness. Man must therefore respect the particular goodness of every creature, to avoid any disordered use of things which would be in contempt of the Creator and would bring disastrous consequences for human beings and their environment" (CCC, no. 339).

ENDNOTES

1. Cf. GS 26 § 2.
2. St. John Chrysostom. *Hom. in Lazaro* 2, 5: PG 48, 992.
3. AA 8 § 5.
4. St. Gregory the Great, *Regula Pastoralis* 3, 21: PL 77, 87.
5. SRS 9.
6. Cf. SRS 17; 45.
7. CA 28; cf. 35.
8. GS 36 § 1.

PRAYER FOR THE POOR

God of Justice,
open our eyes
to see you in the face of the poor.
Open our ears
to hear you in the cries of the exploited.
Open our mouths
to defend you in the public squares
as well as in private deeds.
Remind us that what we do
to the least ones,
we do to you.
Amen.

Excerpts from CCHD website—*www.usccb.org/cchd/neighb.pdf*

Index

125

About the Author

John P. Hogan, Ph.D., has worked with Peace Corps and Catholic Relief Services in Africa, Haiti, and South America. He has taught at Catholic University, Loyola College, and SAIS, Johns Hopkins University. He lives in Washington, DC.